# ALT FOR NORWAY

## Christian Klebo Skjervold II

The Resistance Movement
# IN NORWAY
during World War II

# En må legg en merke efter seg

[You should leave something to remember you by]

# ALT FOR NORWAY

## Christian Klebo Skjervold II

The Resistance Movement
IN NORWAY
during World War II

Edited by Odell M. Bjerkness

BIRCHPOINT
PRESS

Second Edition, 2022

Copyright 2012 by Betsy A. Skjervold

Birchpoint Press

Richfield, Minnesota 55435, USA

Email: altfornorway@gmail.com

Design: Bill Lundborg/Tides Edge Design, LLC

ISBN 978-1-4675-4005-6

Printed in the United States of America

*Cover Photo:* Norwegian resistance fighters coordinate their plans by radio from isolated cabins in the mountains. The resistance movement soldiers wore armbands as seen on the cover photo which shows the Norwegian flag, H with a 7 interposed on the H (Haakon VII) the royal crown and under that "Hjemmevernet" meaning "Home Guard".

The armband shown at the beginning of each chapter was presented to Christian Skjervold by the Director of the Norwegian Resistance Museum in Oslo for his work on establishing the museum.

# ◼ Table of Contents ◼

# ■ PREFACE ■

The family of Christian Skjervold spoke mostly Norwegian on the farm in Westbrook, Minnesota. Later, Christian's proficiency in the language and an interest in the land of his ancestors gave direction to his studies at the University of Minnesota and the University of Oslo, Norway. Christian lived in Norway with his family during the school year 1961-62. He chose the World War II Norwegian resistance movement as a focus of his study and M.A. thesis topic. His research, both at home and abroad, included extensive interviews with resistance participants. He assisted Professor Magne Skodvin, his advisor at the University of Oslo, to establish a permanent collection on the subject at *Norges Hjemmefront musseet* (Resistance Museum) in Oslo. Christian expanded his resistance thesis into a Ph.D. dissertation in Norway during the school year 1966-67 while on a Fulbright-Hayes scholarship.

He then began a 30-year career as a teacher of history and social studies and developing the Ethnic Cultural Center in the Minneapolis Public Schools. He also worked as an insurance investigator in order to support his growing family. But he always found time to be active in the Twin City Norwegian-American community. Because he was an authority and a very engaging speaker, his talks were much anticipated and well-attended. I met Chris in the 1970s and we began a 40-year collaboration on language and cultural history projects that included grant proposals, curriculum studies, seminars, symposia, and four books. During his retirement years the idea for a definitive book on the Resistance Movement took shape. Chris chose the title *Alt for Norway*, from the motto of King Haakon and of the Resistance Movement. In prior years, work on an Emigrant Museum in Ottestad, Norway and collaboration on the American College in Norway at Moss took the front seat.

As Chris's health declined, during the last six months of his life, he and I had several chats to pull together the details for the book you are now holding.

Christian Skjervold died on November 3, 2011. With the assistance of his wife Betsy and family, we finished preparing *Alt for Norway* for publication. To the best of our ability we remained faithful to Christian's intentions for the book.

Odell M. Bjerkness, Editor
Professor Emeritus
Concordia College, Moorhead, Minnesota

# ■ DEDICATION ■

To my wife Betsy;

my daughter Karin,

her husband Brad,

and their son Klebo;

and my son Kristian III,

his wife Jeni,

and their children,

Kristian IV, and Silje.

# ■ ACKNOWLEDGEMENTS ■

I have, in the course of writing this book, received assistance from a great many institutions and individuals. Foremost among these individuals is Professor Magne Skodvin of the University of Oslo *Historiske Institutt*. It was through Professor Skodvin that I came to write on the resistance, using the Majavatn incident as the central episode to illustrate the differences in goals and methods between the Norwegian home resistance and the resistance directed by the Allies. Professor Skodvin has given me much valuable information through interviews and directed me to other sources and persons to interview. A word of thanks is also due Professor Sverre Steen, Chairman of the History Department at the University. Among the institutions that aided my research for this book are the *Historiske Institutt, Universitetsbiblioteket, Nobel Institutt,* and the *Forskningsrådet.* I must thank other individuals who through their association with the resistance movement proved to be valuable resource persons: Jens Christian Hauge, leader of *Hjemmestrykene,* member of *Rådet* and post-war Minister of Justice. Also Erling Grannes on whose farm the Majavatn incident occurred must deserve a special note of thanks. Other notes on sources will appear as an appendix to this book. My special indebtedness to the author of *Hjemmestyrkene,* Sverre Kjeldstadli must be mentioned; for, although Dr. Kjeldstadli died prior to my work in this area, his notes and materials of research preserved at the University of Oslo proved to be invaluable to me in my research. Finally, a word of thanks is due to Kaare Haukaas, curator of the *Norsk Krigstryksamling* at the University library and to private individuals who on their own initiative sent me materials and letters.

Christian K. Skjervold

Special thanks to: Odell M. Bjerkness for his friendship, encouragement and contacts; Pr. Kristin Sundt, Alf Antonsen, and Kristian Skjervold III for assistance with translation; Bruce Tipple, John Xavier, David Smith, Joann Bjerkness for proof reading; Susan Tapp, copy editor; Karin Skjervold for design suggestions; Bill and Linda Lundborg for layout and design; and JoEllen Haugo for indexing.

Betsy A. Skjervold

# ■ FOREWORD ■

When the young Danish Prince became the king of the newly independent Norway in 1905, he took the name Haakon VII. Along with assuming a thoroughly historic name, he told his new kingdom that his watchword or motto would be *Alt for Norge* (All for Norway). He intend-ed to be the champion of all people of his adopted home-land, and through the years he and his family, Queen Maud and Crown Prince Olav, traveled throughout the land to become ac-quainted with the people and nature of Norway.

King Haakon's selection of All for Norway as his motto was prescient in its effect. Until 1940 it served to bind the king to his new land, and after the German inva-sion of April 9th, it became the slogan for a generation of individuals and groups who singly or in concert stood up to the seemingly overwhelming might of the Nazi war machine. *Alt for Norge* continued to be the watchword of the king and royal family as they resisted

■ **The coronation of King Haakon VII in Trondheim's *Domkirke*, (Cathedral Church), June 22, 1906**

the German onslaught by refusing to accept the Nazi occupation as an accomplished fact during and after the invasion. His motto continued to guide the king and the resistance at home in Norway, as well as abroad in England, Canada, and the United States, and in all corners of the world where Norwegian sailors put their lives on the line to enhance the Allied war effort.

Those who saw a chance to profit politically from the occupation – *Nasjonal Samling* (NS) National Unity Party members – were seen as traitors to Norway and were dealt with by the resistance movement during the war and by the nation in a series of trials after the war.

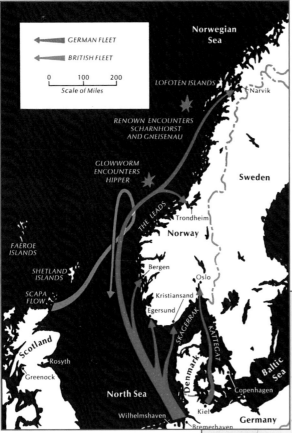

■ The German Nazis launched a six-point attack on Norway: Oslo, Kristiansand, Egersund, Bergen, Trondheim, and Narvik using for the first time in modern warfare the blitzkrieg approach including air, sea, land and submarine forces.

■ Topographical map of Norway, Sweden, Russia, and Finland showing the 26 *fylke* (counties) and the 800 mile border with Sweden

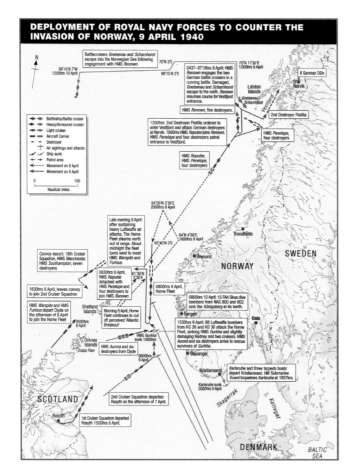

■ Deployment of British and German naval forces for the invasion of Norway on April 9th, 1940

This book is the result of several years of research into archives and interviews with some of the individuals who participated in the resistance to Nazi occupation. The purpose of this work is not to cover all the ramifications of the invasion, war, and aftermath, but rather to open an exploration of the main lines of the resistance to the Nazi occupation.

A common theme voiced by the participants in the resistance, from either the right or the left, was their dedication to Norway. Individuals may have come from disparate backgrounds but when the war came to their beloved Norway they were united in their resistance to the occupation power and those who collaborated with Nazi Germany.

The leaders of the resistance, who have been interviewed were, to a person, united in the sentiment expressed by Peder Furubotn, the leader of the Communist resistance, and Jens Christian Hauge, leader of Milorg. When asked why they risked their lives, each replied, "I am Norwegian."

These men and women gave their all for Norway, meaning in all too many cases that they gave their lives.

# ■ INTRODUCTION ■

The purpose of this work is to examine the main lines of the Norwegian and Allied resistance in German-occupied Norway during the years of World War II. This book will consider the relationship that existed between the Norwegian home resistance, *Hjemmestyrkene,* abbreviated to HS, and the Allied forces working to make Norway a thorn in the side of the Germans. The relationships of HS and the Allies were primarily the relationships that existed between the military arm of the resistance, Milorg *(Militær organisasjon),* and the British Special Operations Executive (abbreviated to SOE) along with the American Office of Strategic Services (OSS). The Russian efforts to aid the resistance were of some importance, but due to geographical and military factors their aid was limited mainly to northeastern Norway and to Communist-inspired activities of a more spontaneous nature in Norway as a whole.

Because Norway was an important British sphere of interest during World War II, the examination of Allied-Norwegian relationships is mainly a study of Anglo-Norwegian conflicts and cooperation. Because the legal Norwegian government was able to influence both the Allied programs for Norway and the workings of the various resistance operations in the homeland, the position of this government, which sat in London, is yet another factor considered in this work.

This book will show that Anglo-Norwegian relations were strained throughout 1940-1941 and the better part of 1942, they improved from late 1942 through 1944, and were particularly good in the last year of the war. It will show that the strained relations that were experienced were a result of failure to coordinate methods of operation and goals between the Norwegian Milorg and similar home-grown organizations, and the British-directed resistance under SOE. This failure to coordinate goals and methods led to more serious consequences than simply misunderstandings and strained relations. Among the serious consequences were the mass arrests of persons connected with both SOE and home resistance groups when plans were exposed by the German *Gestapo* (the *Statspoliti*—abbreviated to *Stapo*), or the German military. The situation became so difficult that Ole Berg, the leader of the home resistance, said that for a time in 1942 he considered giving up. There are many examples that could be used to illustrate the contention of disorganization among resistance groups. In this work the Majavatn incident will be analyzed to show the degree to which SOE and Milorg often worked at cross-purposes with each other. Majavatn has been chosen because it has the essential content to illuminate the differences between the methods of operation of SOE and the Norwegians. Professor Skodvin urged that additional research should be done on this topic, as this would be of benefit to the history of the Norwegian resistance as a whole.

The story of Majavatn will be told throughout this writing, and it will be used to illustrate problems of Anglo-Norwegian cooperation. It will also be shown that Majavatn was one reason for closer working relationships between the Norwegians and the Allies. Further, it will be shown that throughout the entire history of the resistance there was a growth of the resistance from a state of disorganization into a very systematically organized resistance movement.

As to a consideration of the war in general, it would be impossible to discuss the Norwegian resistance movement without reference to the greater Allied war effort and to the European plans of the Germans. It will be shown that Norway was considered to be of great importance by the German military planners, and that the resistance, both SOE and Norwegian, had an effect on the timetable of World War II.

Majavatn, while it is only one incident during a time filled with many events of great significance, certainly deserves to be closely examined.

■ **Majavatn Lake is on the west side of main highway E6, and Majavatn village is midway between the east side of the lake and E6.**

# Chapter 1

## LOVE US OR FEAR US

**In order to understand the events at Majavatn** in late 1942, it is necessary to retrace the events of 1942 that led to what has been called the Majavatn tragedy. Throughout the early part of the war the Allies had attempted landings in Norway, and it was in Telavåg on the west coast in April, 1942, that the Germans first inflicted harsh reprisals in response to these British landings. Goebbels had earlier said of the Norwegians, *"Wenn sie uns nicht lieben lernen, so sollen sie uns wenigstens furchten."*[1] If they won't learn to love us, at least they shall fear us.

In Telavåg the Germans burned more than three hundred houses, butchered or took away all the livestock, ruined all transportation and deported all grown men between the ages of 16 and 65, a total of 76 persons, to concentration camps in Sachsenhausen, Germany. The remainder of the population, 260 persons, was interned in Norway. Many of the women and children of Telavåg lost all that they had – husbands, sons, brothers, home and property. Telavåg was the Norwegian Lidice and Oradour.[2] From Telavåg the Germans followed the trail of resistance work into Trøndelag, where the Germans, after "Operation Redshank" on May 4, tightened controls in the Orkdal area so as to make resistance work almost impossible. Then, in July, the *Gestapo* began arresting Milorg men in the Drammen area of eastern Norway.

After Drammen the *Gestapo* proceeded to Østfold, where the SOE agent "Crow" was arrested on July 26.[3] In August the Communist led resistance in Oslo made an attack upon the NS *Statspolitiet* headquarters on Henrik Ibsensgate.[4] This threw the *Gestapo* and the *Stapo* into a state of feverish activity against all forms of resistance. On the sixth of September the work of the Germans and the Norwegian Nazis became deadly serious in Nordland and Trøndelag, the prelude to a tremendous tragedy in Norwegian resistance history – Majavatn.

Majavatn is in Nordland *Fylke* Grane *Herred,* not far north of Trondheim and approximately 60 miles south of Mosjøen. Majavatn lies on the main highway connecting North and South Norway and is also on the only main railway line north of Trondheim, *Nordlandsbannen.*

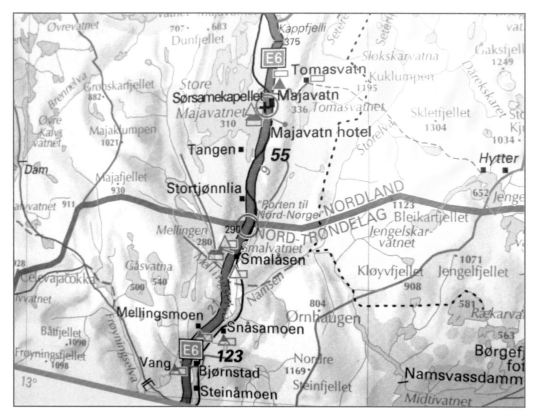

■ Today, Majavatn village has a hotel and extensive camping facilities on the east side of the lake

## British Send Agents to Nordland

Just prior to the New Year, 1942, the British sent English-trained agents to operate in this area of Nordland. The main work of these agents was to organize a military group in the district. Some men were already organized into a home resistance, but the main objective of the British agents was to build a force independent of any Norwegian control. The agents believed that only professional spies or saboteurs, not local civilian leaders, could be trusted to keep quiet about the important work that was to take place. SOE men came to the Vefsn area in Helgeland under the leadership of Captain Sjøberg with code names such as Archer, Heron 1, and Heron 2.[5] They hoped to organize a force of at least 250 persons that would serve, at some future date, as part of a larger force that would "cut Norway in half." It has been reported that Sjøberg and his men told the civilian population that an Allied invasion to liberate at least North Norway would come during the year 1942, as soon as possible.[6] When the Norwegians heard this, they were eager to help in any way they could. Here was a chance for some real work in the war effort; no longer did they have to "lie low and go slow" as they had been advised to do up until this point. The work that the British agents had in mind for the people of the area was to transport weapons from a landing point at Vefsn to Majavatn. There were two ways in which the weapons were to be handled: in one, they were to be carried overland from the head of the Vefsn fjord to Majavatn; in the other they were to be off-loaded at Vefsn from vessels that had carried them from Great Britain, and loaded onto fishing boats to be taken to the docks at Mosjøen. We know with certainty that this operation began in January and continued through the spring and early summer and into July. Many men had been used in the buildup, and approximately twenty-four metric tons of weapons, explosives, ammunition, and supplies had been brought safely in under the very noses of the Germans. An operation of this magnitude seemed to prove the worth of the British agents in Norway. They had safely organized and built up a force capable of assisting a carefully planned large-scale Allied action.

Sometime in the early spring a man known as Hammer joined the work in the Majavatn area. He had been vouched for by a reliable man, Reider Karlsen. Many observers believe that the man known as Hammer was an informer in the pay of the Norwegian Nazi, Rinnan (an agent of the Germans) in Trondheim. In the fall of 1942 Karlsen and Hammer said that they were going to Sweden as they felt things were becoming dangerous in the Majavatn area. These two, shortly after their disappearance, were sought by the police. Karlsen reported to authorities in Sweden, but Hammer was seen, a few days after his supposed flight, walking openly on the streets in Mosjøen.

On September 6, 1942, the ax fell on North Norway. At this time the radio telegraphist in "Archer," Reider Årkvisla, was arrested at Trofors outside of Mosjøen. Henry Rinnan and his people were at the root of the arrests. Since the number of people involved in weapons transportation had been large and the British agents did not have a close personal knowledge of the people involved, it had been impossible to keep the operation secret. Rinnan had, for quite some time, been employing techniques that Kjeldstadli calls *"spill i den negative sektor"* (the negative sector game). These techniques included contact and infiltration, control and leadership, informing, arrests, torture, terror, and murder. Rinnan was a master of all of these techniques.[7] For some time he had his agents-provocateurs placed in the Vefsn-Grane area, and he also employed local informers. The information gathered by these informers and by his second in command, Ivar Grande, filtered into *Sicherheitspolizie und der Sicherheitsdienst Aussenstelle* in Mosjøen.[8]

When Årkvisla was taken, he was subjected to torture, and he was forced to show the *Gestapo* a cache of weapons known to him. The weapons were located on the Tangen farm owned by Erling Grannes at Majavatn. With this the Majavatn tragedy began to unfold.[9]

## Germans Search for Hidden Weapons

In order to reach the farm, the German soldiers had to cross Lake Majavatn. On Saturday, September 5, 1942 as they rowed, with Årkvisla as a prisoner, they were spotted by the men on the farm, Erling Grannes, Erling Jr., Kalle (a cover name), and Hans (also a cover name).[10] Erling Jr., Kalle, and Hans took their weapons and concealed themselves in the woods. The Germans arrested Erling Grannes Sr. and forced him to help Årkvisla uncover the weapons hidden there. The three men in the woods awaited their opportunity; then they opened fire on the Germans. Grannes and Årkvisla managed to escape to the safety of the woods during the firing. Two Germans were killed and two others wounded. While the Germans withdrew, Grannes, Årkvisla, and the other men safely escaped to Sweden, Grannes taking his family with him. Grannes and Årkvisla met again in England. After gathering reinforcements, the Germans returned to Majavatn and searched the entire area. At the time, in a report to the Norwegian government in London, it was stated that the Germans found more arms and ammunition as well as Swedish money.[11]

In the process of searching the area, the Germans arrested about sixty-five persons in Mosjøen and Grane. Most of the male population of Majavatn was arrested.[12] The men in the original roundup were able to hold their tongues. As a result of the secrecy that they maintained, seventeen of the original sixty-five were released. The rest were taken to prison in Trondheim.

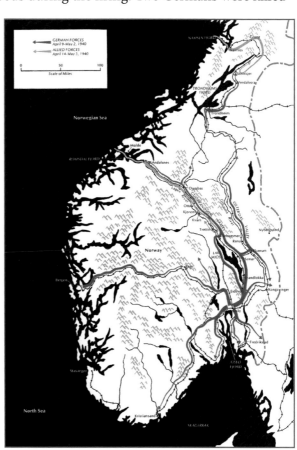

■ **After the initial invasion, the plan was to attack along major roads or rail lines in an attempt to defeat the Norwegian army and to link up their forces on the coastal cities**

On the sixth of October a state of emergency was declared in Trondheim and the area surrounding it, as well as in Grane *Herred*, which included Majavatn. The state of emergency came not only as a result of what came to be known as the Majavatn episode but also from two other SOE-inspired and led operations.[13]

On September 20th the British set in motion an action against a power station in Glomfjord in Nordland. This was the combined Operation Knotgrass-Unicorn with men from Combined Operations, SOE and two men from Kompani Linge.[14] The sabotage itself was a success, but on the way back the resistance members met a German patrol. Of the twelve men, only three escaped. Two were shot at the time of capture and seven were taken prisoner and executed on October 23, 1942.[15]

On the seventh of October, Operation Kestrel of the SOE was put into action. The two men involved were both members of the larger Operation Redshank. These two achieved their objective and were able to reduce the production of vanadium metal from the mine at Fosdalen in North Trøndelag by about twenty-five percent for the next three months.[16]

The Germans were uneasy and had good reason to be. Rumors of an impending invasion by the Allies had been making the rounds of the district. They feared that Majavatn might be the prelude to a full scale landing. Apparently, they knew of Sjøberg's invasion statement and took it at face value.

## Results of Operations

As a result of Majavatn and the other two operations, a state of emergency lasting from the 6th to the 12th of October was declared in the areas. Of the men from the Majavatn round-up, twenty-four were shot in Trondheim on the seventh and eighth of October. A total of thirty-four men were sentenced to death and shot during these six days.[17]

The executions were hard on the resistance movement because of the number shot and the terror inspired among the survivors. During and after this period mass arrests were made. Many resistance people had to flee the country.

Even though the operations at Majavatn, Glomfjord, and Fosdalen were SOE-inspired and had been led and organized outside of Milorg, Milorg suffered a severe setback. Many of its members had helped in Majavatn or had been active in other SOE operations. When the pressure was applied, they were forced to give information detrimental to Milorg.

For the military resistance in District 22 (Trøndelag) and 40-41 (Nordland and Troms) the raids had caused almost irreparable damage. After the shock of the arrests, people did not know whom to trust and, unbelievable as it sounds, Rinnan and his men controlled many of the resistance groups in Nordland and Nord-Trøndelag after the Majavatn episode.[18]

The unfortunate happenings in *Nordland* (North Norway) were coupled with other comparable events in the west, east, and south of Norway. The British-planned Operation Freshman against the Rjukan plant of Norsk Hydro, where heavy water was being manufactured, met with disaster on the night of the nineteenth of November when the glider carrying the operatives crashed into a mountain.[19] The surviving British of the Royal Engineers were executed in January or February, 1943,[20] as the first victims of the Germans new terror tactic, *Kommando-Befehl,* which had been instituted October 18, 1942 on Hitler's order.[21]

Each time a new operation failed, the Germans were able to piece together new information about the resistance movement in Norway. The members of the SOE operations came and, if lucky, returned to England after accomplishing their missions, while the civilian population of the area remained to suffer the consequences. Each time a sabotage action was carried out or discovered, the German pressure and terror directed at the local population grew stronger. The Germans would harass and question the residents of the area and, in this way, gather information about Milorg. As very few locals had knowledge of SOE and other Allied operations, these efforts yielded little information about that element of the resistance. That the Norwegians were mistreated by the Germans as a result of the SOE-directed actions was not a deliberately cruel policy on the part of the British and the Allies, but rather the result of the professional agents' war strategy. What was this strategy? For an explanation of this one must examine SOE and the Norwegian strategy of the Allies in more detail and to do this it is necessary to see SOE from the beginning.

# Chapter 2

## ALLIED RESISTANCE:
## SOE (SPECIAL OPERATIONS EXECUTIVE)

**From late 1939 to 1940 British officials** began to take a greater interest in Norway as an eventual British operations area. Departments of the Foreign office, Ministry of Economic Warfare, War Office, and the Admiralty worked out concrete plans in the event that British forces should be engaged in Norwegian waters or on Norwegian soil.[22] The British government undertook discussions with leading Norwegian industrialists to find out what the Norwegians, such as Norsk-Hydro's Bjarne Eriksen, would do in the event that the output of the mines and industries were to benefit Nazi Germany.[23]

In connection with the British military officials, several undercover "shipping offices" in contact with the British consulate in cities such as Stavanger, Bergen, Ålesund, Trondheim and Narvik were opened.[24] The British naval officers at these offices interested themselves especially in harbors, dock facilities, landing possibilities, railroads, highways, and other diverse subjects of consequence to the movement of troops.[25] Reports from these officers were then sent to the special maritime section of Secret Intelligence Service (SIS).

In reading Churchill's volumes on World War II, one learns that in 1940 the British had been making plans for operations in Norway, despite Norway's declaration of neutrality. According to Churchill, the target date for a landing of British troops in the principal points of Norway was April 10, 1940. The operations were to be launched under the code names 'Stratford" for Stavanger, Bergen and Trondheim and "Avonmouth," for Narvik.[26] Even before this time, in January of 1940, the British hoped to make landings in Norway and even Sweden. In January the Allies had discussed the possibility of aiding the Finns in their fight against Russia. On February 5, 1940, Churchill won a victory for his policy at a meeting of the Supreme War Council in Paris. It was decided to assemble a force of 30,000 to 40,000 men to go to the aid of

■ **German troops march down Oslo's main street, Karl Johans Gate, from the Royal Palace and past Oslo University on the right.**

Finland via Norway and Sweden. As Churchill said, the troops would be sent through Narvik to "kill two birds with one stone."[27] These "two birds" were of course aid to Finland and the cutting off of iron ore shipments to Germany from the Swedish mines at Gellivare via the Norwegian port of Narvik. Preparations were made for the landings to take place in March, 1940. The first British units were to land on March 20 and the French on about March 29, 1940.[28] These plans, of course, never materialized due to the signing of a Russian-Finnish peace on March 13, 1940. With this signing, the moral excuse for an invasion of Scandinavia fell away. Churchill explained, "all of our plans for Military landings were again shelved, and the forces that were collected, were to some extent dispersed. The two divisions that had been held back in England were allowed to proceed to France, and our striking power toward Norway was reduced to eleven battalions."[29]

All during early 1940 the situation continued to deteriorate. On February 16 the British stopped the German transport *Altmark* in the Jossingfjord and released some three hundred British prisoners. This was in line with a British memorandum of January 6, 1940, sent to the Norwegian Foreign Office. The meaning of the memorandum was clear. The British government was "taking appropriate dispositions to prevent the use of Norwegian territorial waters for German ships and trade" and for this purpose it would ". . . be necessary for the British naval forces at times to enter and operate in these waters."[30] This was an open threat to Norwegian neutrality.

## German Preparations to Invade Norway

Long before open British threats to Norwegian neutrality, the Germans were secretly preparing for operations in Norway. The Germans looked to the long coast of Norway with its multitude of good ice-free harbors and remembered the lesson learned in the First World War, i.e., it is not sufficient to have a large force of submarines; it is also necessary to have facilities to repair, re-supply, and, above all, unleash the submarine "Wolf Packs."

In the middle of January, 1940, Hitler seriously considered the occupation of both Norway and Denmark in order to exploit their territories. By the end of January details were being worked out by the General Staff and on February 21, 1940, the implementation of the plan was entrusted to General Falkenhorn.[31] Toward the end of March, 1940, the decision to invade Scandinavia, before the Low Countries, was finalized.

■ **German soldiers land on Norwegian soil in a coordinated attack with the five other Norwegian seaport cities at 4:20 a.m. April 9 1940**

The troops that had been assembled for this operation left Sletten on April 3, and the main body of war ships sailed toward Scandinavia on April 6, 1940.[32]

Even with changes in plans, the Allies maintained their interest in Norway. On March 28, in the Supreme War Council, they approved the laying of mines in the North Sea and Norwegian territorial waters — the leads — to prevent Germans from using those waters as a safe route home for ore from Narvik and to prevent another *Altmark* affair. The mining of the leads was to be accomplished by April 5, but on April 3 it was postponed until April 8, at which time Allied troops were also to be sent to Narvik and to the Swedish frontier.[33] Troops embarked in Britain on April 6-7, but were ordered disembarked on April 8, when it became known that German ships were on their way to Norway.[34] British ships steamed to Norway in an attempt to head off the German invasion by the use of sea power.

When the German invasion of Norway became a fact on April 9, 1940, the Allies were powerless to stop the general advance of the German armies. General Ruge, the Norwegian Defense Chief asked England for help and Chamberlain answered: "We are coming immediately and in full force."[35] Churchill concentrated on Narvik. As he said in his work: "Narvik was my pet." This little town had become an obsession to the British who had fought so long against the ore exports. In his *History of the Second World War,* Churchill explained that German industry was mainly based upon supplies of Swedish iron ore which in the winter flowed through Narvik.[36] Churchill felt that the best summation of his thinking was made by General Ismay on April 21 when he said that the main objective of the Scandinavian campaign was the possession of Narvik and the railroad to the Gellivare mines.[37]

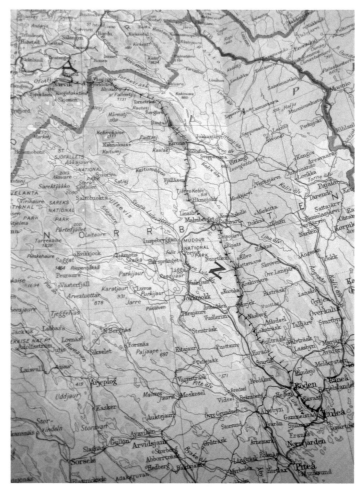

■ The main railroad line carrying iron ore from Swedish mines went up to Narvik in the winter and then the ore was carried by ship to Germany. In the summer when the port of Lulea was free of ice, shipments were made though the Gulf of Bothnia.

The British sent agents into their shipping offices, Narvik, Captain J. Watt Torrance, Trondheim, Major Palmer, Bergen, Captain Croft and at Stavanger, Captain Malcolm Munthe. These men reported to the Military Intelligence Research (MIR) in London that they had not had a chance to complete their mission, which was to prepare for British landings in those areas.

## The British Policy and the SOE

The promise that the British were coming in full force was not realized. The British came and there was some hope that the war in Norway could be won by the Allies. The Allies recaptured Narvik, but for only a short time. However, the contacts that the men in the shipping offices had cultivated were valuable for later resistance work.[38] Three of these men came to work for SOE during the war. Palmer was captured by the Germans, precluding any further activity on his part. Beside these men, the SOE was able to make use of some of the British officers who had been in the campaign in Norway and had some knowledge of Norwegian conditions.[39] The campaign also had given the British contacts with people who later could be called upon by the SOE. These were men, such as Lauritz Sand, Hjalmar Steenstrup, Johnny Pevik, Leif Tronstand, and others who took part in the British-organized home resistance throughout the summer of 1940.[40] It should be pointed out that these were not SOE men; rather they were Norwegians anxious to do something for Norway.

■ **German soldiers set up roadblocks throughout the country with curious citizens looking on**

To understand its work, the entire scope of SOE's goals and operations must be considered. SOE came into being in response to Germany's successful invasions. Even though there were some Allied successes, the German occupation of Norway became a fact in 1940. In the summer of 1940 the British lost their foothold on the continent. On June 4 the last troops left the battle-seared beach on Dunkirk, leaving behind the majority of the expeditionary corps' heavy weapons. On June 8 the last British also left Norway. The armistice between France and Germany on June 22 left England with the feeling of Wordsworth's words from the Napoleonic wars:

Another year, another deadly blow,
Another mighty empire overthrown,
And we are left, or shall be left,
Alone, the last that dare to struggle with the foe.

Churchill felt that defeatism had conquered the French. He vowed that this could not be allowed to hobble the British initiative. Active resistance, not passive holding operations, would be the answer. Great Britain had to find agents in the German-occupied countries. Britain must organize special departments that could direct raids against the German-occupied coast from England.[41] On June 12, 1940, Churchill appointed General Sir Alan Bourne to the Directorate of Combined Operations to carry out such raids. He immediately set in motion the training of volunteers and the planning of such operations. On July 17, 1940, Admiral of the Fleet Sir Roger Reyes was named as the head of Directorate of Combined Operations (DCO) with Bourne as second in command.[42]

Churchill felt that these raids should be carried out by "striking companies" as he called them, which would follow the "butcher and bolt" (hit and run) principle. The goal of these companies, later to be called the "commandos" was to ensure that the Germans on the continental coast from North Cape to Bordeaux were kept in a constant state of agitation. In all, ten striking companies were set up in the summer and fall of 1940. They consisted of men from the Regular Army and Royal Marines, even though Churchill had had to argue long and hard to convince the Regular Army and the War Office of their usefulness. From a Norwegian standpoint, the commandos are of special interest, for Churchill says that they came into being in Norway in April 1940.[43] The first SOE groups came to the Sognefjord and Hardangerfjord areas of West Coast Norway in May, 1940 to disrupt German communications of all types in those areas. Also, Special Forces made up of Norwegians had been used to hinder the German advance from Mosjøen to Narvik.[44] When they returned to Great Britain, these forces were given special training at bases in Scotland and Northern Iceland. Later more companies were set up, one of which is of special interest for this paper: Norwegian Independent Company Number 1, better known as NORICE or simply *Kompani Linge* (named for Lt. Martin Linge). The Independent Companies were later called Special Service Battalions and later still, Commandos.

As background for the British work in Norway, SOE was set up officially in July, 1940 and in August it received its charter.[45]  The charter consisted of the following points: SOE should cooperate  with the Chiefs of Staff Committee.

1—It should animate people to active military resistance.

2—It must seek to lead and supply the pro-British military resistance organizations in German-occupied countries.

3—It should train resistance groups in sabotage and guerilla warfare.[46]

In carrying out its charter SOE was to play a decisive role in Norwegian resistance history.

■ **King Haakon and Crown Prince Olav in the city of Molde during a pause in German bombing, 1940**

SOE came under the Ministry of Economic Warfare as a special department. The Scandinavian division of SOE was looked upon as a separate part of SOE and came under the leadership of Charles Hambro, later Sir Charles Hambro, K.B.E. SOE's first operation on Norwegian territory was carried out by a Norwegian force from Aberdeen, Scotland via Shetland at the end of May, 1940.[47]

## Different Methods of SOE Operation

All through the summer of 1940 young Norwegians came to England by whatever means they could. Some came across the North Sea in small boats while others came to England from wherever in the world they found themselves to be before the German occupation. Many of these volunteers were contacted by SOE Scandinavian Region through J.L. Chatsworth Munsters and P.W.I. Boughton-Leigh. In September, 1940, Lt. Martin Linge came to England and was named by the Norwegian government to work with these two men in recruiting Norwegians for SOE. On December 22, 1940, the first SOE-trained secret agents were sent to Norway under the code name "Vita."

In an effort to distinguish the different methods of operation employed by the SOE, one can look at three loosely defined phases: sporadic, organized, and systematic.

■ **Resistance fighters blow up German railroad administration building in Oslo**

The reader should keep in mind that the definition of these three phases is "very loose" and that many times during the course of the war even the most carefully trained agent or the most carefully planned operation seemed to belong more to the sporadic phase when its impact was considered.

The commando raids by the Independent Companies in 1940 and the resistance actions in North Norway can be classified as sporadic. They were "thrown in" to do something, to cause disruptions that could potentially delay or stop the German advances. Unfortunately, these actions were too few and were launched too late.

After the Germans had secured military possession of Norway, a new strategy was called for. The British came to realize that the sporadic raids were a failure; they then set about sending in agents with training for special missions. In October, 1940, Sir Charles Hambro set up an SOE division that would work out of the British legation in Stockholm.[50] This special department would set up a shuttle operation for sending agents into Norway from Great Britain. Sabotage was to be approved by SOE in London before action.[51] The agents would go to Norway by boat from the Shetlands, and leave Norway via Sweden, and then home by plane or vice versa.[52] This type of action constituted the beginnings of the organized phase of the resistance. "Vita" was the first example of the organized phase, occurring at the same time as Malcolm Munthe in Stockholm tried to open contact with the home-grown resistance in Norway to stimulate them to action against the Germans.[48] He was able to open the channels of communication through people he had met in Norway during the time he was the "shipping agent" in Stavanger. The most important point of this phase was that the operations assured the Norwegians that the British did want to help liberate Norway.[49]

The third phase of the SOE program was being planned while agents were being sent to Norway. This third phase can be said to have its beginnings in 1941, with the raids against the coast of Norway, mainly north of Trondheim. These raids were carried out by the Directorate of Combined Operations in cooperation with SOE. From these beginnings the systematic phase would continue throughout the remainder of the war.

A great deal of SOE planning went into these raids before they were carried out. Churchill himself was strongly interested in the outcome of the raids, and he was quite anxious to see them succeed as a means of providing a possible shot in the arm for general morale, as well as a means of making military progress. It was hoped that the Allies might regain a beachhead in Europe. The raids of 1941 were well-planned by the British, but the SOE failed to take the Norwegians into their confidence. This failure, as will be seen, created larger problems than those that were solved by the raids.[53] The raids themselves were of two types:

▶ The first type had as its aim the destruction of anything of value to the Germans with as little loss of life to the attacking forces as possible.

▶ The second type consisted of active warfare with the goal of engaging the Germans in battle.[54]

An example of the economic type of warfare was Operation Claymore against the Lofoten Islands in 1941. The first raid of this operation began on the 4th of March, and the expedition, codenamed Rebel, received a warm welcome from the patriotic Norwegians in the Vest-fjord area. The main objectives of the expedition were to destroy fish oil production, sink shipping, and arrest Norwegian Quislings, *Nasjonal Samling* (NS) members. Another objective was to allow as many patriotic Norwegians as possible to go to England and continue the fight from there. In line with the general economic warfare directives for Operation Claymore the expedition was a success:

▶ 1900 tons of shipping were destroyed

▶ 18 factories were ruined

▶ 3,000,000 liters of oil rich in vitamins A and D and valuable in the making of explosives went up in smoke

▶ 213 Germans were taken prisoner

▶ 12 NS members were arrested

▶ 314 Norwegians were able to leave to continue the fight from Britain.[55]

The forces met no serious resistance and withdrew at 1:00 p.m. with, as Martin Linge put it, "The sound of a thousand voices lifted in *Ja vi elsker*" (the Norwegian national anthem).[56]

Churchill was pleased with the results and sent his warmest congratulations to the chiefs of Combined Operations (CO).[57] Here was a British success, a British offensive that had achieved a goal of value to the general war effort.

The active-type of warfare was exemplified by the raids (Operation Anklet and Operation Archery) against the Lofoten Islands on the 26th-28th of December, 1941, and against Måløy-Vågsøy on the 27th of December, 1941. These raids could not hope to retake Norway nor even North Norway, but they

■ **In December 1939, Vidkun Quisling meets with Adolf Hitler and begins discussing Quisling's claim that the British intend to invade Norway**

would be like the prick of needles, irritating the Germans, and perhaps causing them to spread their coastal defenses thin so that at some point a landing in force could be accomplished. Of course, the raids could serve Allied propaganda and the Allied war effort as mentioned before. Looking at these raids closely, one can see more clearly exactly what they accomplished, keeping in mind that these raids helped to shape Anglo-Norwegian relations, which were to become critical in 1942. One can also see how they follow a general British pattern that became all too evident in Majavatn in September, 1942.

# Chapter 3

## ALLIED SCANDINAVIAN POLICY

**The Rebel operation in Vestfjord was a success,** to be sure; it had destroyed material of acknowledged value to the German war effort. However, some of the 52 Norwegians participating in the aid began to have some doubts about their role. They were still Norwegians, even though they operated from Britain, and the material that had been destroyed in the operation was Norwegian, not German. The British saw northern Norway as only one operations area in a total war and their resources had to be used to Allied advantage. While the Norwegians may have agreed with this general viewpoint, they also saw Northern Norway and the Lofoten Islands as part of their mother country.

Who had given the command that sent 52 Norwegians to Norway to destroy Norwegian property? The British, of course, were responsible. This raised another question of concern to the Norwegians. Was it right that Norwegians stood under British command and carried out British planned operations when Norway was still technically a free and independent country with a responsible government, including functioning entities that concerned themselves with war and defense, i.e., a defense department, *Forsvarsdepartementet* (FD) and a military command, *Forsvarets Overkommando* (FO)? These were questions that needed answers. The Norwegian soldiers asked themselves whether the Norwegian government in London had known of and approved the raids. Had their government approved the methods and objectives? These questions became even more nagging when it was learned that the Germans had made reprisals against the civilian population as a result of the raid. These questions were answered by an SOE document that stated that almost all of the Norwegians in Norway and Great Britain, including King Haakon were strongly in favor of such raids. In this document of April 16, 1941, entitled "Scandinavian Policy," the SOE leaders presented an overly optimistic picture of the situation regarding Norway.[58]

The basic conclusions in the "Scandinavian Policy" document were sound in that they recognized the fact that conditions for the civilian population were very difficult. Food shortages were growing worse as a result of the demands placed upon the economy by the occupation troops. It also mentioned that as a result of forced productivity the industrial potential was wearing down. In other words, very little machinery had been replaced since production facilities were turned towards the manufacture of war material. The document went on to explain that as a result of the demand placed on them by the occupation, the Norwegians' will and ability to resist were in danger of weakening. Therefore, because of diminished morale and physical well-being it was hoped that Norway would not be forced to live through another winter under occupation. Optimistically the document went on to state: "It therefore behooves us to do all in our power to see that Norway is liberated before Christmas of this year, 1941. In order to do this it will be necessary to set in action as many raids of the Lofoten type as possible and as quickly as possible because summer with its short nights will soon be here, or else raids would be postponed until the fall."[59]

■ **German infantry soldiers transport supplies to the center of Oslo on April 9, 1940**

To carry out this policy, it was necessary to institute a program that would involve people who were familiar with Norway and Norwegian conditions. As a result of the success of Operation Claymore and the thinking that went into "Scandinavian Policy" in April of 1941, the British committed themselves to train 20-50 Norwegians each month to work for SOE.[60] The training program was set in operation and the aforementioned Captain Martin Linge was named as the Norwegian representative. As a result of cooperation between Captain Linge and Colonel J.S. Wilson, Norwegian Independent Company Number 1 *(Kompani Linge)* was set up in July, 1941, as a part of the Norwegian Army, but under British command.[61]

## Nazi Germany Invades the Soviet Union in 1941

Another element, which comes to play an important part in the consideration of Norway as a factor in the entire war, enters the picture at this point. On June 22, 1941, Hitler broke the Molotov-Ribbentrop Pact which had formed the basis for if not cooperation, at least non-aggression, between Nazi Germany and the Soviet Union. It is known that the new German Army that had been built up prior to the outbreak of war had had a base in Northern Russia, *Basis Nord*, located not far from Murmansk. The Germans had been allowed to use this base from October 10, 1939, in accordance with the August friendship pact. When the Germans invaded Norway in 1940 and were able to secure all of Norway, including the North, they no longer had any great need for *Basis Nord*. They withdrew through no charity on the part of Hitler, but because the Russians had, on April 5, 1940, placed very harsh restrictions on traffic through the base.[62] On September 10, 1940, they gave up the base.

When Norway was invaded in April, fighting did not cease immediately. On June 17, 1940, just over a week after the active war was over, Terboven the *German Reich-kommisar Norvegen* (Reich Commissioner of Norway) flew to Kirkenes in Finnmark, North Norway, to raise the swastika flag even though there were still Norwegian troops garrisoned there.[63] The question can be asked: "Why was it necessary for so high a personage as Terboven to travel such a great distance to raise the Nazi flag?" The answer lies in the direct collision of German and Russian interests in three European areas: the Baltic, the Balkans, and northern Norway. Russia grabbed the Baltic nations first, so this collision was solved temporarily. When Italy entered the war on Hitler's side, it was hoped that would secure the Balkans for the Axis powers. In order to keep Russia out of North Norway, something had to be done quickly while the Red Army was still occupied with other problems; hence, the symbolic flag-raising served to warn Russia that this was a German sphere of interest and that she would tolerate no meddling. An additional factor was that Hitler, in all likelihood, knew that the friendship of 1939 could not last and therefore hoped to secure another jumping-off point against Russia.

When the final Nazi-Soviet break came in June of 1941, Russia's other allies, Britain and later the United States, would find that the most practical way to supply Russia was through the ports of Murmansk and Archangel. In order to transport material to these ports, it was necessary to pass the north coast of Norway. The Russians set forth a plan to go into North Norway and drive the Germans out, but the British were not in agreement with this plan. However, the British realized that with Norway under German occupation convoy traffic would be subjected to heavy attack by both German

■ **The German Gestapo assumes control of Victoria Terrasse, formerly the Norwegian Foreign Ministry building**

aircraft and U-boats. Therefore, the British entered upon a plan to establish a "half-permanent" base either at Bodø or on one of the islands nearby.[64] In the program set forth in "Norwegian Policy" of December 11, 1940, and "Looking Ahead in Scandinavia" of April 15, 1941, SOE stated that it hoped to build up a force in the Bodø area that could cut Norway in half in a wink.[65]

This desire to cut Norway in half was held by many of the foremost British leaders, among them Winston Churchill. It was hoped that this plan would be feasible because the northern half of Norway could present the Allies with a valuable base on the continent. This would also ease the pressure on the supply lines to Russia in the east. During the course of the war this hope was expressed several times and in several ways, both orally and actively, and the first attempt to initiate this program was made in December, 1941 with Operation Anklet.[66]

## Måløy and Vågsøy

Until the fall of 1941 most of the raids on the Norwegian coast were, as the Germans named them *Nadelstiche*, or in English, pinprick raids, that were of minor military worth.[67] On October 27, 1941, Captain Lord Louis Mountbatten became Director of

Combined Operations, with which SOE cooperated. Lord Mountbatten shortly thereafter was named Acting Vice-Admiral, titular Lieutenant General in the Army and titular Air Marshall of the Royal Air Force (RAF). His title became Chief of Combined Operations and embedded in this title there lay the germ of a strategy, the use of all three branches of the military in big raids to make for faster and more effective operations than ever before.[68] The raids that employed this new approach included Måløy-Vågsøy, Bruneval, St. Nazaire, and the last, Dieppe.

We shall consider the Måløy-Vågsøy raid, Operation Archery, and then look at Operation Anklet. On December 26, 1941, the first of the big combined raids was launched. The objectives were to cause as much damage as possible in the Måløy-Vågsøy area in Nordfjord, with as few losses as possible.

The hope of being able to complete the task without a fight proved impossible. There were in the Archery force 576 officers and men. Of the 576 there were 15 men from *Kompani Linge*. The raid was carried out on December 27, 1941, with success as far as destruction was concerned, but the battle was hard on the raiders.

■ **Vidkun Quisling begins a propaganda campaign with a poster reading "With Quisling—a New Norway"**

Martin Linge was killed along with twenty others, and many were wounded. Even with the comparative success of the raid, a jarring note could be heard among the local population. "There was a great deal of dissatisfaction with *Kompani Linge* because of the destruction of Norwegian property and the fear of reprisals against the civilian population."[69] Martin Linge had been killed in the attack on the German headquarters on Vågsøy. Prior to this time Linge had more than once smoothed things over and dampened the "jarring note," but now he was gone and the dissatisfaction had returned.[70]

■ **Minister President Quisling and Terboven, German appointed Reichskommissar (state commissioner) to Norway, meet in Akershus Fortress to plan future cooperation and to begin a propaganda campaign**

At the same time as Archery, Operation Anklet moved against the Lofoten Islands. Anklet lasted from December 26-28, 1941 and proved to be a great disappointment to the Norwegians. The plan called for the establishment of a semi-permanent base in the Bodø area or one of the islands nearby. When Anklet came to Reine and Moskenes in the Lofotens on December 27, 1941 the expedition had 300 men including 77 from Kompani Linge under Major J. Watt Torrance. All 300 were under the command of Rear-Admiral L.H.K. Hamilton. The force met no resistance on landing and was welcomed by Norwegian patriots. However, a few of the locals expressed their feelings in this way: "You are welcome if you are here to stay, but we do not wish for a new Svolvær." This was a reference to the raid of March 4, 1941 at Svolvær that had caused the Germans to strengthen the security in the area and institute a stronger coastal defense. These actions were accompanied by reprisals and more restricted freedom for the civilian population.[71] The British assured the Norwegians that they had indeed come to stay and many Norwegians, eager to help with liberation, gladly loaned their boats to help in any way possible.[72]

Rear Admiral Hamilton had planned to stay a while. However, when he learned that the Germans were gathering strength to attack his beachhead, he decided to withdraw. Suddenly and practically without warning, Anklet left the Lofotens. The expedition took with it 266 Norwegians who were to go to England. They also captured six NS members and took them to England. However, in retribution for their help to Anklet, the stay-at-home Norwegians suffered reprisals from the Germans in the form of "Minister" Fuglesangs *jossing-lister* (enemies lists).[73] These reprisals became known to the men of *Kompani Linge* and it was not easy for the British to make them understand that Hamilton's actions were necessary.[74]

The military expeditions came and then sailed away again. The Norwegians had to stay and face the repercussions. Certainly the withdrawals were excusable on military grounds, but when one was subjected to the reprisals that followed, it was understandable that the raids created mistrust on the part of the Norwegians, both at home and abroad.

## Historic Milestones of British Raids on Måløy-Vågsøy and Reine-Moskenes

The British raids against Måløy-Vågsøy and Reine-Moskenes marked a milestone in wartime occupation history in general and for the history of the Norwegian resistance more specifically. The operations in themselves were of small military value to the British. However, they were the cause of many important political and military decisions in the first part of 1942. In the political field, Major Vidkun Quisling had been pushing for more power throughout 1941, and he hoped to get it at a ceremony at Akershus Fortress in Oslo in January, 1942. He hoped to make Norway independent and to have Terboven called back to Germany. He said that if NS got free reign it would make Norway a loyal partner in the new Europe. After Quisling held complete power, peace negotiations would take place between Norway and Germany. Quisling hoped to take power on January 30, 1942, Hitler's birthday, but this was not allowed. Instead, the date was moved to February 1, and this was not the only change Hitler made. Quisling received the title, Minister-President, but very little real power.[75] Hitler considered Norway as the decisive landing area, *das Schicksalsgebiet in diesen Kriege* (destinies area in this war) according to Admiral Raeder.[76]

Hitler was certain the Allies would attempt to establish a base in Norway, quite possibly at Andøya, because here it would be easier to build the necessary airfield.[77] Therefore, it was out of the question for Hitler to waste valuable time supporting Quisling, a man known to be of dubious popularity in Norway, in a governmental experiment.[78] Hitler felt that Norway was the invasion area, and he waited for the coming invasion of Norway until well into 1943. He even felt that the American-British landing in North Africa in the fall of 1942 was just camouflage for the real landing in Norway. In accordance with these beliefs, he strengthened the occupation forces from 100,000 – early 1942 to 250,000 men in the summer of the same year.[79] From December, 1941, the primary strength of the German Navy was stationed in Norway.[80] From Grand Admiral Raeder we learn that Hitler, in answer to the raids of 1941, sent the *Scharnhorst, Gneisenau* and *Prins Eugen* up through the English Channel to the North Sea, which "created the greatest British maritime sensation since the Spanish Armada."[81]

The British and Norwegian raids carried out in 1941 had consequences beyond the purely military. The Germans were not able to strike back at the SOE and the British; therefore, they took revenge on the Norwegian civilian population and intensified the campaign to stamp out the home-grown resistance organization. All through the year 1942 the Home Front tasted the bitter fruits of the raids, until at last the Majavatn tragedy and its consequences occurred.

# Chapter 4

## MILITÆR ORGANISASJOENEN (MILORG)

**The name Milorg has been mentioned** several times to this point but with no more than a hint as to what it was and what its objectives were. The name Milorg was the abbreviation for *militær organisasjonen* (the military organization). It was the section of the Home Front that took upon itself, in a positive way, to do something about the German occupation of Norway.

In order to understand Milorg and its viewpoint, we have to go back to the complex period directly after the invasion of April 9, 1940. On the one hand, many Norwegians were shocked into passivity.[82] It took time for the real significance of the occupation to sink into the collective mind of the Norwegian people. On the other hand, there were those who saw immediately what needed to be done and did all in their power to resist militarily. There had been, of course, a mobilization call that had been announced before the Germans took over all communications. Failing to reach their designated mobilization centers, some went to the forests and mountains on skis or on foot to

■ **As many as 10,000 copies were printed of one issue of an illegal underground newspaper, *Kongsposten*, (The King's Mail)**

find a military unit so that they could be of some help to the resistance. Many of these volunteers were the ones who later helped to form the rank and file in Milorg.

At 7:30 p.m. April 9, 1940 Vidkun Quisling read a proclamation over Norwegian Radio naming himself the leader of the government as prime minister. Quisling said that Prime Minister Nygaardsvold had lost his position. Quisling said further that his new cabinet urged the people to maintain calm and order and that further resistance was "not only futile but the same as criminal ruination of life and property." Also, he announced that every Norwegian, especially those officers in the Army, Navy, and Air Force, was bound to accept orders from the new "national government" of the NS party.[83]

■ **King Haakon and Crown Prince Olav inspect Norwegian military units training in England**

That further resistance was futile was not self-evident to many Norwegians. As mentioned earlier, when the fighting was over, a number of patriots hid their weapons to wait for a better day. "During the war and shortly after its official close there were in Notodden and the surrounding districts, organized small groups that promised to stay together and not to recognize that the war was over even after Norway was occupied and weapons had been laid down." These groups were joined by mobilized and volunteer soldiers who, in a belief in the "new front," had not delivered up their weapons at the surrender, but rather hid them for later use. "These groups were already gathering in the summer of 1940 but each group stood alone. At this time one was not aware of a nationwide organization, but one believed that in all certainty there would be one someday."[84] All over Norway the same type of activity occurred. Another example can be seen in the report signed by Vidar Smalås of the home forces in Namskogen, Nord-Trøndelag just south of Majavatn.[85]

■ The British ship HMS *Duke of York* engages in a battle with German vessel *Scharnhorst.*

The will to resist received vitalization and legitimacy through appeals from King Haakon and from the defense chief, General Ruge. "The people must hold out, they must carry on the resistance. The day would certainly come when Norway once more will be free."

General Ruge's speech in June, 1940, expressed the resistance viewpoint in this way: "Remember this: a state cannot rise again just by waiting until something happens —that help shall come from outside. It must be ready to help itself when the time comes. It can take time for that day to dawn, but it can also come faster than one could believe today. Therefore, I urge you to help each other in your own way, to hold this thought warm until the day comes. It can come faster than anyone believes. Wait, Believe and Be Ready."[86]

## Reasons for Milorg's Growth

Wait, Believe, and Be Ready—each in his own way: these are the key words for an understanding of Milorg's growth over the whole of Norway. Those who took the initiative were from all walks of life and from all groups. They came from rifle clubs, sports clubs, youth groups, and labor unions, and a long list of other clubs and

■ **German carpet bombing levels the west coast city of Kristiansund**

organizations. In just the north of Norway it was reported that at least 2,000 rifles and carbines were not turned in when the official military resistance ceased, and the same source states that the Vefsn Rifle Club had about 850 active members in 1939.[87] Those who were interested in resistance work went quietly about their community and organized small circles, talking person-to-person to friends and acquaintances. Most of those in the armed resistance at this time were men who had had some experience in the army or army reserve.

The resistance movement was built one piece at a time, not in a mass production manner. Each man would be hand-picked and the leader would know the next man he chose to work with him. If a Milorg man was not able to hold his own, he endangered those around him. There were those who would join just to do something interesting and, as always, there were those who were loose-tongued. Some people have maintained that the Norwegians themselves were the *Gestapo's* best friends. In conversations with people who had personal experience with the Majavatn case, many of them mentioned that there were those Norwegians who were so happy to be doing something to fight the war that they just could not help telling the world about it, even if there happened to be informers' ears in the crowd.[88]

On the whole, however, the *lagfører* (platoon leader) knew the people in his group. He knew one from school days, another from work and a third from a club he belonged to. He often knew men from years before and perhaps their parents and grandparents and therefore could depend upon them. He knew who had good physical and mental stamina and he was able to select only those who he felt would not break under stress.

The *lagfører* knew he must set a good example for he asked much and could offer little. A man in the Milorg group had to sacrifice his personal life to a great extent. He had to provide his own clothing and equipment and at least eight days' food rations. He could not tell anyone he was in Milorg. He had to promise to be present for military instruction when the platoon leader requested. He received no compensation for lost time or use of personal effects. He knew very little about his own Milorg group, and he received no information on Milorg's leadership. In other words, he received only such information as was necessary for him to carry out a task assigned to him. Therefore, most Milorg members were not in the secret army for glory or as soldiers of fortune, but to be with, and do something for country and people. Most felt that this was payment enough.[89]

This thread of a desire to do something for the country was common from the small, manifold, local independent resistance groups to the central, unified, national organization.

# Chapter 5

## MILORG'S GROWTH
## AND NATIONAL ORGANIZATIONS

**In connection with Milorg's growth,** it should be pointed out that Milorg served a dual role in wartime Norway. Local and centralized voluntary associations played a key role in the growth of the military resistance.

Norway is a long, narrow country and is often sparsely populated, but all of the more settled areas had their own associations for the promotion of skiing, soccer, marksmanship, etc. In addition, most of these groups had national contacts in the capitol of Oslo, such as *Nordlendingensforening* (North Norwegians Association) or *Vestlandslaget* (West Norwegians League). These associations served as points of contact for people of like interests or similar backgrounds. The chairman of one group knew the members and, at the same time, might know twenty-five chairmen of other voluntary groups. In this way, each individual member of a club had the basis for a network of contacts in many other groups.

For the resistance movement this network of organizations proved to be of immeasurable value. The Germans would disband groups and then the Norwegian Nazis would attempt to organize them along National Socialist lines, but they could not stop the old friendships and personal ties. The Teachers Association *(Norges Lærerlag)* and the Doctors Association *(Lægeforeningen)* could be placed under new Quisling leadership, but the Nazis could not prevent individual members from organizing resistance among the teachers or doctors. For Milorg this personal contact was of vital importance. The many small threads of contact throughout the land were gathered and woven together into one strong rope from individual to group to district to *Sentralledelsen-SL* (Central Leadership) and Rådet (the Council, governing body of Milorg) in Oslo to Forsvarets *Overkommando-FO* (Defense Command) and the Norwegian government in London.[90]

■ **The German scorched-earth policy destroyed over 1,000 buildings in the Finnmark area as shown here in Vadsø**

Of all the voluntary groups that contributed to Milorg's resistance efforts, the sports clubs did the most. They were the best organized and had members in every nook and cranny of the land. They also had had experience in organization and in cooperation. Without a doubt, in 1940 the sport clubs were the single most important factor that pushed the military resistance forward in thought and deed.[91]

It was not until November of 1944 that the resistance movement's three main groups were gathered under common leadership for the first time. Sivilorg (the Civil Organization) led by *Kretsen* and *Koordinasjonskomiteen* (KK-the Coordination committee), Milorg led by *Rådet* and *Sentralledelsen* (SL), and *Polorg* (the police organization) under *Politiledelsen*, were all gathered under *Hjemmefrontensledelse* (HL-Home Front Leadership). It was HL in cooperation with the Norwegian government that led the resistance fight to the time of liberation.[92]

In HL the resistance movement, in 1944, reached a goal that the diverse people and groups had set for themselves in the fall of 1940, under the name *Hjemmefronten* (the Home Front). The task was to organize a permanent and national organization . . . in close cooperation . . . with the government.[93]

It was only natural that the first activity of resistance groups should be centered in Oslo, for it was here that the German occupation forces and the Quisling government both had their seats of power. It was also here that what was left of the legal pre-war government remained–such as a few members of the *Storting* (Parliament) and the Høyesterett (Supreme Court). It was in Oslo that one had the best chance to organize resistance against the rules and laws of the Germans and the *Nyordning* (New Order), the Quisling and German reorganization of Norway. For these reasons the Oslo group, very early, attained a central position in resistance work. For these and other reasons, Milorg looked to Oslo for leadership as the war progressed.

## King Haakon Asked to Abdicate but He Refused

The Germans and Quislings unwittingly gave the resistance a great deal of help when on June 27, 1940, the *Storting* asked King Haakon to abdicate. The problem of how to deal with the king had been under discussion for some time and it had been suggested that if the king did not abdicate voluntarily, he would then have to be deposed. However, the Storting's President did not want to close all avenues and, in a letter of

June 18 to Terboven and Hitler, the president said that the possibility of offering the crown to Prince Harald should not be closed off forever. The "Harald letter" further expressed the hope that German wisdom in this case would lead to a growth of friendship between Norway and Germany.[94]

King Haakon on July 3 answered the request of June 27

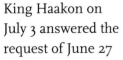 **King Haakon sends inspirational messages to Norway from London on the CBC radio**

by saying that, since he had been freely chosen as king in 1905, he did not believe that the request for his abdication was an expression of a general desire but was the "forced result by a foreign military occupation power."[95] The status of the king and the royal house led to a whole series of problems. The Germans and the Quisling government kept pressing the *Storting* for more and more concessions, until finally on September 18 the people who were dealing with Terboven and Quisling could no longer see their way clear to compromise and the negotiations fell through. The last blow came on September 25 with the "Iron fisted" *Nyordning* speech by Terboven. He proclaimed a new order for Norway. The king was declared deposed and the new government of Norway was to be led by Quisling and the *Nasjonal Samling*. This speech was a clear turning point in the history of the Norwegian resistance. At last, each individual Norwegian had a clear choice. You were either for the king or against him. Some followed Quisling, and the membership of the NS grew in the following period.[96] However, the majority remained loyal to the king and government in London, and it has been said that "practically the whole of the Norwegian people were united in resistance to Quisling and the occupation Power." The resistance movement had a rallying point–something that they could gather around: the person of the king. By the last days of 1940 the Oslo group of the resistance had planned, at least on paper, resistance in Oslo and over the entire land.[97]

The men who planned the first resistance groups came from all walks of life. Many were from the Norwegian Officer Corps who had been taken prisoner and put in the concentration camp at Grinni, outside of Oslo. The names are too numerous to mention, but Captain Johan Rognes and Major Olaf Helset were two who did a great deal to organize the resistance movement into a logical structure. Helset became a traveling inspector for *Nasjonalhjelpen* (National Help), an organization to assist in local conditions of need and in this way was able to camouflage his activities that took him around the country to make resistance contacts.[98] Gradually, the authority of the men who had done the original foundation work grew. There was not, in the first year, a sharp distinction between the men who worked with the civil resistance, military organization, or the military intelligence segments of the resistance. The same men or the same group of men could conceivably work in all three areas. Here the British had a valid criticism of the Norwegian method of doing things. The British criticized the overlapping of duties and responsibilities.

With respect to this issue the Norwegians came to agree that the British were right. The activity of the *Gestapo* and the military *(Abwehr)* in the first year of resistance work showed the Norwegians that they should specialize more and try to build a series of independent cells—water-tight compartments, so to speak, so that no one man knew more than necessary about the resistance organization. The change led to less direct contact between groups. This ensured that if one man was taken or had to flee Norway, the entire organization would not be crippled into the future.

After the first trial year the general resistance became more specialized due to compartmentalization. The civil resistance received as its special field a national holding campaign—"not let the NS gain ground—do not let people become apathetic." The military organization worked to build a secret military organization with the thought of fighting some day. The military intelligence or espionage network became independent of Milorg, except for special groups and individual persons, and was gathered under what became known as XU.[99]

By the spring of 1941 the military resistance had grown extensively, resulting in greater complexity of leadership and administration. The groups had become wider in scope. It was for the purpose of finding a more effective method of dealing with problems that Jakob Schive, Ole Berg, and Johan Holst decided to call a meeting of the leaders of Milorg. The meeting took place in late April or early May. In addition to the three men mentioned, Lasse Heyerdahl Larsen, Arne Kogh-Johanssen, Viggo Widerøe, and Johan Gørrissen were at the meetings. These men set about to organize a military council for Milorg. They agreed that this council, simply called *Rådet* (the Council), should be Milorg's highest authority and serve as its leadership. The first two members of *Rådet* were Ole Berg and Johan Holst.[100] During the early summer of 1941 the building of Milorg progressed at an increased tempo.

The local groups were strengthened and coordination became a reality. It was loosely reckoned that there were between 20-25,000 men in Milorg, even though the leaders were aware that many were "paper soldiers."[101] *Sentraledelsen* (the central leadership) had established contact with the SOE in Stockholm under Malcolm Munthe. Contact had also been established with the Norwegian Legation in Stockholm as well as with the Norwegian government in London where one of the original Milorg leaders, Johan Rognes, was engaged.[102] In addition to the enhanced coordination and communication, the financial condition of Milorg improved significantly in 1941. It received money from private sources in Norway and some funds from the government in London. At one time Foreign Minister Koht's courier brought some 60,000 kroner.[103]

## Political Legitimacy Lacking for Milorg in 1941

However promising the situation may have been for Milorg in the early summer of 1941, it lacked one essential ingredient. That was formal approval by the Norwegian government and the king. Formally, Milorg was a private army with no legal standing, and the leadership of Milorg struggled with this lack of official sanction. With formal approval by the king and government the authority of Milorg and Rådet would be greater. The energy and activity created by Milorg could be more easily channeled and with greater specificity. Also, Milorg had to coordinate its actions to complement those taken by the Allied military forces. They had to have a general overall view of the aims and objectives of the wider war, and the aims of Milorg had to be transmitted to the Allied military leaders. An ill-planned or ill-timed sabotage action by the Allies or Milorg could have very serious consequences for the entire character of the resistance because of the potential for German reprisals against the civilian population. The liquidation of a dangerous informer could lead to the shooting of innocent

Norwegians. These issues plagued the Milorg leadership. Had they the right to take upon themselves the sole responsibility for resisting the Germans with a private army? After all a capitulation agreement had been signed on June 10, and the Norwegian Army had agreed not to take up arms against the Germans.[104]

The work of Milorg and Rådet was made more difficult by the three-way split in the direction of resistance by Britain, Milorg, and the Norwegian government. Milorg's leadership was often divided on the worth of the British activity in Norway. It often felt itself weighed down by the British objectives, methods, and agents. The British car-ried out their work in Norway independently of Milorg and the Nygaardsvold govern-ment. The British gave their agents orders to work outside of Milorg and with as little contact with Milorg as possible. So long as Milorg was character-ized as a private army, the British in SOE and SIS could neglect Milorg without fear of harming relationships with the Norwegian government in London.

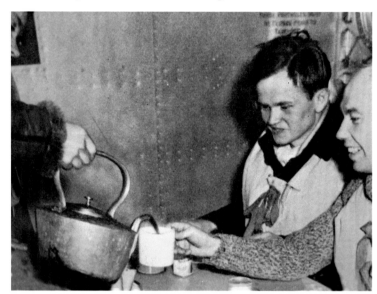

■ **Real coffee, not chicory, put smiles on faces of resistance fighters**

The only way Milorg could shed the character of a private army was with the seal of approval of the king and the Nygaardsvold government.[105] Perhaps most importantly, Milorg could not carry out physical military resistance without military material. They also needed Allied invasion troops and Allied weapons that of necessity had to come from the outside—from the Allies via the Norwegian government.

These and other similar concerns were in the minds of Milorg leaders when they sent a letter to the king on June 10, 1941.[106] *Rådet* here, in short, gave the outline of the buildup of Milorg and said that until later the main goal was to consolidate the organization. For the time being they wished no weapons and took a position of com-plete abstinence from sabotage acts, as these would only sharpen the watchfulness of the enemy. The expressed policy of Milorg was to "go slow and lie low." This policy irritated the British. A former Milorg leader called Milorg a "military Sunday school"

■ **Grini Concentration Camp near Oslo is one of several that together held over 20,000 Norwegian men and women**

and he, Rognes, advised the Nygaardsvold government that Milorg was something that money would be "thrown away upon."[107] The June 10 letter also prompted a reply on July 17, 1941. This directive criticized Milorg for not establishing contact with resistance elements in North Norway and scolded them for a failure in organization north of Trondheim. "We are aware that the population of Narvik is especially anti-German and that great hatred of the enemy exists very generally in northern Norway if only as a result of the reprisals that followed the Lofoten raids."[108] Therefore, it would be valuable if Milorg could send suitable people to the north to organize reliable men into a group to be "run independently but parallel to the organization in the south."[109] The British went on to explain that it was necessary to bring supplies of weapons into Norway long before any planned general activity in order to facilitate training in the use of weapons. Also, they took the position that acts of sabotage were necessary and that it was only the unskilled use of sabotage that was dangerous, as skillful sabotage could be made to look like a genuine accident. The last paragraph of this report sets the tone of the British attitude:

Further, it must be clearly understood that it will not be for any governing body in Norway to decide when the military machine now being created is to function. This can only be done by the Officers in Command of the Norwegian Forces in the United Kingdom acting in conjunction with and under the direction of the British General Staff.[110]

The rather sharp tone of the message quoted above was prompted by the June 10 reference to a national leadership *Kretsen* (the Circle) that appeared to some in the government in London as an attempt by the resistance to set up as an extra governmental agency in competition with the government in exile. The Nygaardsvold government had reason to be skeptical of the events in Norway, as they knew that they had been blamed for the unfortunate mobilization and for fleeing to England. The government knew that it was the person of the king who provided the rallying point both within and outside of Norway. In order to placate the resistance groups, one of their members, Paul Hartmann from *Kretsen,* was named to the government on December 19, 1941.[111]

The government further defended its actions by saying that it was only right that the cabinet, king, and crown prince had left the country. This action prevented the same sort of situation as existed in Denmark and also upheld the sovereignty of Norway. Also, the fact that the legal government of Norway was in England made Norway a partner with the Allies. This later made Norway's transition into the post-war world much easier. However, during the early years of the war the government in London was under sharp criticism from many sides, including pressure from both the Home Front and the British.[112]

Already in May of 1941 the Norwegian Foreign Minister, Trygve Lie, had signed a military agreement with Britain which allowed that all Norwegian forces in Great Britain should be allied with and under British command.[113] Therefore, the British looked upon the conflicts between *Rådet* and the Norwegian government as a Norwegian-British problem, rather than a purely Norwegian issue. As a result, it was the British who formulated the rather sharp letter of July quoted above. In the final analysis, the July letter was not so much an answer, as a directive, which is clearly explicated by the last paragraph, "This can only be done . . . with and under the direction of the British General Staff".[114]

*Rådet* was not able to answer the July directive immediately due to some arrests of Milorg men and problems of communication over the North Sea. It was not until October that *Rådet* was able to get into contact with the government. When the Milorg representatives reached London, they found out that Trygve Lie had not told the other cabinet members of the British directive nor of the original Milorg letter. Prime Minister Nygaardsvold was, to say the least, personally displeased by this.[115]

# Norwegian Government in Exile was Unclear on Problems at Home

It is easy to understand that the government, which had been in a foreign country for over a year, did not have full comprehension of the problems at home. It is even clearer that misunderstandings would grow in a situation where communication was stopped by one of the governmental ministers in cooperation with the British. However, to the government's credit, it saw that Milorg presented a problem that could not be solved by merely ignoring it. The government needed to take a position. Most arguments were for approving the actions of Milorg and giving it the seal of approval as an official arm of the Norwegian military. After the war the *Undersokelseskommisjonen* (the Parliamentary Investigation Commission) stated the problem in a most concise way. The main thoughts were these: (1) that the military work in Norway be coordinated with the general war policy, as Norway is one of the Allies and therefore could not allow an independent military group in Norway; (2) that the government was in a serious situation due to the secrecy of the resistance, for it might unwittingly be furnishing aid to persons hostile to the Norwegian government. Another question was the type of activity *Milorg* should undertake, passive buildup for a final assault, or active guerilla and sabotage warfare. The government could withhold a decision but it was strongly bound by British and Allied policy.[116]

The consequence of the October meetings between the representatives of Milorg and the government was a telegram outlining a Defense Department decision of November 20, 1941. The government recognized the military organization in Norway and its leadership represented by *Rådet*. "All who fight for Norway's freedom at home are to place themselves under the organization Milorg."[117]

The government's approval of Milorg and *Rådet* was the first big obstacle cleared from Milorg's path. Milorg was now the fourth line of defense along with the Army, Navy and the Air Force. *Rådet* now had concrete authority both at home and abroad and Milorg was the only approved resistance group at work in Norway. Milorg's members were now formally, not only voluntarily, under military command. Importantly, Milorg could depend on military help from outside. However, the kind, amount, and time of delivery would still depend upon the British view of the war and on Milorg's effectiveness. Also, the new approval led to a degree of cooperation between the British and Milorg.

There were still weak spots in Milorg's organization. Much of the criticism that the British had leveled at Milorg in the July 17 letter was well-deserved. As Sverre Kjeldstadli points out, there was a large gap in Nordland and the resistance in Nordland County *(Fylke)*, was placed under Milorg as D4C on the Milorg map under *Sentralledelsen*. Late in 1944 and into 1945 the work picked up speed under the *Districktaledelsen* (district leadership) and played a role after liberation in helping the many prisoners of war who the Germans had concentrated there. Troms County, to the north of Nordland, lay on the periphery of any resistance work, and Finnmark was always outside of Milorg's domain.[118] This problem of North Norway was one of the reasons for the Majavatn tragedy in 1942. The two significantly different strategies characterized by Milorg (go slow and lie low) and SOE (hit and run) were responsible, in the main, for the mass tragedy at Majavatn.

We now can see the cross currents that affected the relationships of the three forces in this wartime triangle, SOE, Milorg, and Norwegian government. The misunderstandings of motives, methods, and objectives led to conflicts that could not be resolved overnight. At times it was not just simple misunderstanding, but rather mistrust and uncooperativeness, which hampered the work in Norway, particularly prior to the end of 1942. The problem that shall now be considered is inextricably intertwined with the aforementioned, and that is, who was to have mastery over the effort expended toward the one goal on which all parties could agree, the freedom of Norway and the defeat of Germany?

# Chapter 6

## THE CONTROL OF NORWAY

**Until the late fall of 1942** the military resistance in Norway was hampered by differences of opinion and operational styles between the Norwegians and British. These differences were already in evidence during the campaign in 1940. The difference as to methods and aims became deeper after the military defeat of Norway and its occupation.[119] From a Norwegian point of view, British prestige had been weakened. The British regarded the Norwegians as plagued by defeatism. Many of the British who had been in the Norwegian campaign joined SOE in London and Stockholm, and some maintained that the Norwegians were not suited to take part in secret resistance. They felt that Norwegians had to learn the hard lesson of security and they had to learn it in the bitter school of experience. The Norwegians, they maintained, were too open, too naive, and too talkative.

The leaders of SOE were even skeptical of the Norwegian military men in London and Stockholm. The SOE said that the military men in London were not even interested in military information from Norway. From London, then, it was the British, through the SOE, who first began secret military resistance work from outside of Norway.[120]

The British felt that the Norwegian legation in Stockholm was a center of defeatism and that the Norwegian military there was not interested in encouraging resistance work among the young men who had fled Norway and had come to Stockholm seeking leadership and assignments.[121] British skepticism concerning the Norwegians led them to work through SOE to build a secret resistance in Norway, independent of the Norwegian officials in London and Stockholm, and independent of the resistance growing under Milorg. SOE, therefore, sought to build upon proven contacts—men who would accept the leadership of the British. Further, the SOE had to try to come into contact with individual Norwegians in high positions. They hoped that if they could influence highly placed Norwegians SOE might be able to control, through them, the actions of the Norwegians. Even when SOE did get into contact with Trygve Lie and

Birger Ljungberg, they did not provide them with complete information. Trygve Lie states that he had been working in cooperation with Economic Warfare and Sir Charles Hambro ever since he had come to England. However Ljungberg, the defense minister, and Nygaardsvold were both somewhat skeptical of the British plans.[122]

It has been shown in the previous chapter how SOE grew in the early phase of the war. By the fall of 1940, SOE Scandinavian Section had its own office in the British Legation in Stockholm. It had, in cooperation with SIS, opened the Shetland Base. It had begun training Norwegian SOE agents. It had established contacts in Norway and even carried out some actions there, and had also established some SOE-led groups in Norway. By the end of 1940, the SOE felt that it could formulate some long-term goals for Norway and

■ A U.S. editorial cartoon comparing Viking warriors to modern Norwegian soldiers appears in the *Washington Post*

these were stated in "Norwegian Policy" of December 11, 1940.

## The SOE's "Norwegian Policy"

For an analysis of "Norwegian Policy" we must turn to Sverre Kjeldstadli in his book *Hjemmestyrkene*. "Norwegian Policy" began with a discussion of the strategic possibility of guerilla warfare in the future. It mentions that SOE Scandinavian Section could plan on military action in three circumstances: (a) an Allied invasion of Norway on a large scale, (b) assisting the Directorate of Combined Operations (DCO) raids which hit and run, and/or (c) an attack from the air. SOE leadership felt that for Norwegian liberation the first strategy would be the most reasonable. As a large scale Allied invasion might take time, one of the main aims of the SOE was to bolster Norwegian morale by propaganda and successful sabotage. The goal was to ensure that the Germans never felt secure. The most important aim of SOE was to be able to instigate a massive folk uprising all over Norway on a moment's notice. For this separate organizations were needed over the whole of Norway, each with a competent leader. They were to be in contact with each other and with SOE via Stockholm.

"Norwegian Policy" gave a long list of detailed instructions to the leaders of local groups. The leaders were to pick "good Norwegians," i.e., loyal Norwegians who had no reason to be suspected of any Quisling associations. They were to attempt sabotage at their place of work. They should attempt slowdowns or try to ruin machinery and tools. If DCO commandos attacked, the groups should do their best to cut communications from the affected area, and if Germany invaded England they should attack communications and transportation so as to hinder troop movements. SOE asked this not only for Great Britain's sake but also for the sake of Norway. The explanation was that the only way Germany could win the war was to defeat England and by helping England loyal Norwegians would be helping Norway as well.

"Norwegian Policy" further says that at that time in Great Britain there was a secret organization that had good contact "with the best elements" in the Norwegian government in London. This, of course, was Mr. Trygve Lie. The report goes on to say that the leaders in Norway should know that SOE would do all in its power to supply weapons, radios, explosives, and other equipment. Also, it would train Norwegians to be instructors in work necessary for resistance. SOE asked in return that the groups in Norway send all available information on German troop movements in Norway. This last point was something that greatly interested Churchill. He said, "It is of course urgent and indispensable that every effort should be made to obtain secretly the best possible information about the German forces in the various countries overrun, establish intimate contacts with local people, and to plant agents. These, I hope are being done on the largest scale . . . by the new organization."[123]

"Norwegian Policy" went on to say that as far as North Norway was concerned, in all probability there would not be any use for any such organization. The situation appears to have changed drastically between the writing of "Norwegian Policy" and September of 1942, when the Germans found quantities of stored weapons in Majavatn. Perhaps the British hoped that the major raids directed against the Nordland coast in 1941 would solve the problem of German occupation in that area. In any event, the British changed their position between December 11, 1940, and the time they sent agents into the Helgeland district of Nordland *Fylke* to try to organize a force of some 200-300 men. However, the Norwegian Policy excepts the Bodø area of northern Norway. The report stated that SOE needed a strong organization in that area, which should have training in guerilla warfare.

The aim of this guerilla organization was to cut Norway in half when the Allied invasion came and the uprising would begin. In addition to Bodø the SOE wanted to concentrate on the main towns of Norway: Stavanger, Drammen, Trondheim, Bergen, Kristiansand etc., except Oslo. In Oslo, the report claimed, there was more of a willingness to go along with the "New Order," and also there was the other organization that had to be handled on "somewhat special lines." "Norwegian Policy" included instructions to the Norwegians to go all out to help the saboteurs who from time to time would

■ **Destruction in Finnmark is so extensive that some people have to live under a large, upside-down boat with no windows or light**

come to Norway. It stated that it would be wise for these saboteurs to avoid the local Milorg groups completely. The saboteurs were special, not like the ordinary resistance people, as they had specialized knowledge and were effective in their work.

In closing, "Norwegian Policy" explained that SOE's program in Norway contained, "Long Run Aims and Short Term Aims." The first was that SOE should train and equip local resistance groups in Norway. These should have as their goal, to augment an Allied invasion of Norway. Until then these groups should not do anything but train and be ready. The short term program built upon the fact that the SOE, in the time prior to an invasion, should be active through sabotage in Norway and at all times cooperate with the Directorate of Combined Operations and give its support to hit-and-run landings and air raids.[124]

## SOE Leaders Want to Go Their Own Way

The leaders of SOE were energetic and anxious to help the Norwegians in their resistance to the Germans, but they wanted to do it in their own way. They were impatient with the seeming passivity of the Norwegians. The British did not appreciate the deep shock that the Norwegians had received when they were invaded. The Norwegians had hoped that if they acted as neutrals they would be allowed to remain neutral. There had been the feeling "it can't happen here" within Norwegian society. However, the will to resist became stronger after September 25, 1940, when at last, the Germans completely broke the framework of law and justice within which they had, to a certain extent, operated prior to that time. One can see therefore that, compared to SOE, Milorg got a relatively late start, and thus it built more carefully and was less aggressive in its policies.

This is not to be held against the Norwegians, for they had to live day-to-day with the unreasonable rules and regulations imposed by the occupying force. They also were aware of the terror tactics of the German *Gestapo* and NS terror organizations. They knew of the reprisals that were carried out after the Lofoten raids in March of 1941. They also knew of reparations that were extracted from a community if a German installation was damaged. The Germans steadily sent out notices of the strong punishments that would befall anyone helping the British or engaging in resistance, and the Norwegians knew of many people who were arrested merely on suspicion of wrongdoing.

SOE was aware of the fact that the Norwegian home resistance was growing throughout 1941, but still did not want to have too much to do with it. What contact it had with Milorg was mainly through the Norwegian officials in London, and SOE was not anxious to see Milorg grow as a centralized agency for the resistance. SOE wanted to build the watertight compartments and to lead them directly from London and Stockholm. They believed that the wisdom of this approach was confirmed when in the fall of 1941 Milorg was hard hit by arrests in Oslo, Bergen, Trondheim, and other areas of the country.[125]

The activities of the British in Norway had, for some time, given the leaders of Milorg reason to believe that the cooperation between SOE and the Norwegian government in London on the question of the military resistance in Norway was problematic. The reply directive which *Rådet* received to its communiqué of June 10, 1940 only served to deepen his impression.[126] As mentioned earlier, when Schive came to London in October he found out with certainty that the government, as a whole, had known nothing about the reply that had been drafted by SOE.

British reaction to the formal approval of Milorg by the Norwegian government on November 20, 1941, was not long in coming. On November 24, 1941, SOE issued a memorandum entitled "Anglo-Norwegian Collaboration regarding the Military

Organization in Norway." This memorandum was written and sent by Sir Charles Hambro to Defense Minister Oskar Torp. SOE expressed a strong desire to cooperate with the Norwegian government and with the Norwegian home resistance movement. SOE said that it fully appreciated the Norwegians' desire to stand under Norwegian command.[127] SOE could well go along with these desires, but first they had to be certain that the work in Norway would progress along lines that had been drawn up for resistance work in the other Nazi-occupied countries.

The report asserted that the British could not operate in Norway without Norwegian help and the Norwegians could not operate without British help. Therefore, a committee should be established. Hambro suggested that an Anglo-Norwegian Joint Committee should be set up in London with direct connection to *Rådet* in Norway. This committee would also have direct radio contact with the leaders of the individual districts. In order to diminish the danger of one man knowing too much, Milorg should give up its centralized organization patterned after the regular army. SOE also wanted to control communication between the Norwegian officials in London and Milorg. Communications should not go from London to the Norwegian Legation in Stockholm and then to Oslo but rather through SOE hands at the British Legation. As a final gesture of cooperation the British said they had nothing against Norwegian Independent Company Number 1 *(Kompani Linge)* being incorporated as a part of the Norwegian Army, but it would remain under British command to carry out those operations for which it had been trained.[128] Under Norwegian command *Kompani Linge* might not be sent out on operations that might cause unfortunate results for Norwegians.

Before the year was out there was a great deal of dissatisfaction within *Kompani Linge* as a result of the raids of December. This dissatisfaction focused on:
‣ recall of the Lofoten expedition
‣ potential reprisals to civilians left behind
‣ a feeling of helplessness and isolation from Norwegian authorities due to the death of Captain Linge
‣ regret over the absence of any responsible Norwegian officer at the training base
‣ fear that they were being used in a way to bring them into disfavor with their own king and government[129]

Not only was there dissatisfaction within *Kompani Linge* but there was also bitterness within the Norwegian government. Foreign Minister Trygve Lie wanted to know who was responsible for the raids and why he had not received prior information. In regard to the Lofoten raids, therefore, he had to deny any sort of responsibility on behalf of the Norwegian government.[130]

At the beginning of 1942 the period of the raids culminated. The workings of the various operations that came to the west coast of Norway have been discussed in the chapter on Milorg. There is not much more to say of the raids except that from the foregoing one can see why 1941 ended on a sad note and that the jarring note, when the consequences of the raids led to destruction of Norwegian property and fear of reprisals among the civilian population, had been heard once too often. If the period ahead was to hold any promise at all, there would have to be more cooperation between the various bodies interested in the liberation of Norway.

# Chapter 7

## THE GERMAN OCCUPATION AS A FORCE TO RECKON WITH

**Up to this time the discussion** has focused mainly on the cross-currents among the groups that worked for Norway's liberation in the dark days before the hinge of fate swung toward the Allies. The workings of the German occupiers must also be considered.

Action taken by German police in the occupied countries was initiated by the *Gestapo*. The Nuremburg trials stamped the *Gestapo* as a criminal agency that had received the express power to take action outside the law in the occupied territories. In the main, it was the *Gestapo* and *Sipo u. SD* (*Sicherheitspolizei und Sicherheitsdienst* — the police and intelligence-gathering organization responsible for repression of the local population and for the persecution of the Resistance, Communism and the Jewish population), which fought the resistance movement and made life miserable and unsafe in occupied Norway.

There was a strong tendency to exaggerate the role played by fifth columnists in Norway prior to April 9, 1940. We can, in most instances, discredit the occupation period references to mass fifth column movements as being due to hysteria or propaganda. With all certainty, we can ignore the once popular notion that General von Falkenhorst was in Norway disguised as a merchant in women's clothing for a long time, prior to April 9. However, there was a grain of truth in these concerns in that the first chief of Department IV, *Gestapo* in Norway, was Dr. Knab who, since the end of 1930, had been in an undercover position at the German Legation.[131]

In considering the role played by the Quisling NS, it is true that it had contact with the German Nazi party (NSDAP) since the middle of the 1930s, but it was in no real position to give great aid to the invasion since they had no way of knowing when, or even if, it would come.[132]

■ Max Manus and Roy Nielssen, active in Kompani Linge and Milorg, used mines to sink the German troop and munitions ship Donau

The *Gestapo* was divided into several sections, each of which had a special function to carry out. The section that was set up to combat Milorg was IV1b, and the counterespionage section was IV2b. Section IVS (*Sonderreferat*) had the special task of coordination and assessment of the size and activities of the resistance movement.[133] Another very important Section was IVN, which led the entire information service for the *Gestapo*. This section built up a network of agents and provocateurs that infiltrated the resistance movement to provide IVN a glimpse into the plans and organization of the resistance.[134] The beginnings of *Sipo u. S.D.* in Norway in April, 1940 were very modest; but as the occupation period progressed and the Germans saw the general resistance strengthen, new departments and sections were set up to meet the situations.

Throughout the spring and summer of 1940, *Sipo u. SD* worked to gather information under *Gauleiter* Josef Terboven who had the highest authority over all the German police forces in Norway. Then, in the early fall, Terboven reopened negotiations with the Storting to try to find some sort of government that would be acceptable to the Norwegian people.[135] It has been said, that *Sipo u. SD* was against the setting up of a Quisling (NS) government and that instead the Administration Council which had carried out the duties of government should be given full competence.[136] However this was not to be, for on September 25, 1940 the problem grew out of hand and Terboven made his iron-fisted speech discussed earlier.

September 25, 1940 was a demarcation date. The time before had been an attempt at a quasi-legal government. Now plain, naked power took control. Norwegian resistance grew and *Sipo u. SD* increased its activity along all fronts. *Ministerialrat* Berghold has put it thus: "The *Gestapo*, which until September 25, 1940 had shown itself to be comparatively restrained, began from that time its reign of terror, which woke increasing resistance and thereby in a great degree led to sharp consequences."[137]

The *Reichskommissar* Terboven was a man who wanted more personal control. He did all in his power to follow the directive of April 24, 1940, in which he had received full power over all the police in Norway. He rapidly set about bringing the NS police under his control, and he managed to do this on October 25, 1940. He also wanted to expand his power even at the expense of the military under General von Falkenhorst. He said that it was to be his police organization which would lead the fight against the Norwegian resistance.[138]

## Nazi Germany Sharpens Dealings with Norwegian Resistance

As 1940 stretched into 1941, the German dealings with the Norwegian resistance were sharpened. The Germans were concerned with the attack on the Soviet Union and could not tolerate resistance in the occupied countries. The sentences handed down for resistance increased in frequency and in severity. The number of death sentences increased. The Germans were also concerned about the British raids on the coast, and many a civilian from the area of the raids was sentenced to death.[139] This tendency showed itself clearly after the Lofoten raid of March 4, 1941. The hysteria over the British raiders led to retributions, burning of houses, deportations, and stiff sentences imposed upon the civilians. The consequences of the raids, measured in terms of increased *Sipo u. SD* activity were felt over the whole of Norway.

The Norwegians who were found guilty of hindering the German activities in Norway were not even judged or punished under Norwegian law, but under German military law. Norway, according to the Germans, was a German operations area. There was a long list of crimes for which a man or woman might lose his or her life or be sentenced to a long jail term, e.g., writing critical letters, sabotage, illegal photography, helping enemy prisoners of war to escape, illegal use of radios, weapons, and explosives. In general, anything that was against German interests was considered a serious crime.

From the summer of 1941 it became common for the *Sipo u. SD* to employ torture techniques when dealing with captured resistance workers throughout Norway. The hard blows which torture and the new activity of the *Sipo u. SD* inflicted on them frightened but did not stop the resistance. In fact, the opposite was the case. More and more joined both the military and civil arms of the resistance.[140]

On June 22, 1941, Germany invaded Russia. This action came as a stimulus to the resistance in all the occupied European countries because now Germany would be otherwise occupied. Also, the beginning of this new war unleashed a sharp attack from the communists in all the countries involved and in Norway as well. Another factor was that the German Operation Sea Lion (against Great Britain) was not put into effect, which led to hope of greater things from England. Even the United States showed itself interested in a German defeat.

Perhaps the main reason for the more stringent action on the part of the Germans was their fear of an Allied invasion in Norway. In connection with this concern, the *Chef der Sipo u. des SD*, Reinhard Heydrich, came to Oslo.[141] He found several faults with the *Sipo u. SD* work in Norway. It had not been successful in working its way into the resistance organization, and in general had not worked systematically enough. In answer to these criticisms, Terboven set in motion some devastating actions from September 10-16, 1941. He was, in the main, responsible for the shooting of Viggo Hansteen and Rolf Wickstrom and for the lengthy imprisonment of 25 others. Also, he was responsible for the arrest of about 120 men in connection with the milk strike of September 8 and 9, 1941, that was a spontaneous protest against the milk rationing announced on September 8. Other serious consequences of Heydrich's visit included the confiscation of all radios by the Nazis.[142]

However hard Norway was hit by the *Gestapo* measures of late 1941, Milorg was hit the hardest. *Sipo u. SD* was out to break Milorg. In addition, the Milorg work was so large and widespread that it was inconceivable that some of it should not be traced by the *Gestapo*. A false sense of security had permeated the organization in the early days of the war. Milorg had not been on its guard and Nazis had infiltrated the organization. Norwegians had faith and trust in their countrymen and some were too open and talkative. The Norwegians were not accustomed to secret work and many made little attempt to cover their activities. Each individual had contact with persons in other groups and perhaps carried out several different activities. There were no watertight compartments. There was also a mistake in organizing Milorg along the same lines as the Army, namely into five divisions: Østlandet, Gudbrandsdalen with Østerdalen, Sørlandet, Vestlandet, and Trøndelag. It should also have been clear that the lack of cooperation between Milorg and SOE in itself was dangerous for all military resistance in Norway. As long as these two organizations were uncooperative, they created dangerous situations for each other.

As early as 1942, however, each group attempted to find out just what actions the other group was taking. A representative of the Milorg group in the northernmost part of Nor-Trøndelag was named as a liaison man to establish contact with the SOE-directed men operating in Nordland. This Milorg man was the troop leader of Smalåsen Troop District 22-2. His main aim was to establish contact with the agents who had come to the Majavatn area in Nordland *fylke*. He was, however, warned by his immediate superior to avoid giving these men any information as to the strength of membership of the Nord-Trøndelag Milorg. The reason for this warning was that Milorg felt the British agents and the *Kompani Linge* men were too well known in their areas and that they carried on their work in much too open a manner. This difference of opinion as to how best to carry on the resistance was, as mentioned before, a point that hindered the work of both groups. Cooperation between the two groups was almost nonexistent.[143]

At this point the place of Norway in the picture of the entire war must be considered. In the following chapter the plans that Germany had for Norway will be discussed. In connection with this it is well to recall that Hitler personally felt that Norway was the place where the Allies would try to establish a beachhead in Europe. Also it is well to keep in mind the great weight that Winston Churchill placed upon the areas of North Norway, and Narvik in particular.

# Chapter 8

## ALLIED AND GERMAN PLANS

**The British began to work out** detailed plans for the re-conquest of at least part of Norway in the fall of 1941. There had been prior attempts at invasions but the raids during the fall and winter of 1940-41 had been of little military consequence. When the United States entered the war on December 7, 1941, the plans for an invasion were accelerated. One reason for this speedup was that Russia had also joined the Allied side, and the convoys laden with arms for the Red Army passed the north coast of Norway. This made them subject to attack by Norway-based German submarines and planes. Secondly, the United States was strongly interested in opening a second front, which Stalin hoped would relieve the pressure on the Soviet Union. The German leadership and Hitler personally were convinced this new Allied combination made for increased likelihood of an Allied invasion in North Norway.[144]

Everything in the war up to the beginning of 1942 seemed to show that Hitler was right in his personal analysis of the situation: Norway appeared to be the invasion point; the British raids in Lofoten and the Allied alliance with Russia only served to strengthen Hitler's belief in this idea. Even when some of the highest members of the German military tried to tell Hitler he was wrong, he would not listen to their advice. Raeder, several times throughout the winter of 1941-42 tried to persuade Hitler that the Mediterranean area was in the greatest danger of invasion.[145]

Hitler gave orders to strengthen the German Army and Air Force in Norway and to direct the Navy to look toward the defense of Norway as their major concern in the months ahead. It was for this reason that the German fleet stationed at Brest was moved to Norway at such great risk. On the 11th of February, 1942, the American military attaché in Vichy received word from Brest, "They're Gone."[146] By the end of 1942 the most important ships of the German fleet were assembled in Norway.

■ On April 20, 1944, a Dutch ammunition ship enters Bergen harbor and explodes, blowing the roof off the historical Haakonshallen and the medieval Hanseatic houses.

The defense of occupied Norway could not be carried out solely by sending the German fleet to the Norwegian fjords. Land forces were also needed. The invasion of Norway had been carried out by comparatively small numbers of troops. The German Army was so under-manned that they did not have the personnel to prevent Norwegian soldiers living south of Trondheim from passing through the city by rail to assembly points north of the city. When the action was over, the Germans remedied the situation. By the time Hitler was ready to attack the Soviet Union, there were about 180,000 soldiers in Norway. This figure fell as troops were moved to the eastern front, and by January 1942 there were only about 100,000 troops remaining in Norway. Hitler then repositioned units into the "invasion area in this war" so that by June 1942 there were approximately 250,000 troops ready to ward off an attack on Norway.[147]

Not only were troops necessary to defend Norway, but once they were there, some means had to be found to move them around the country as the situation demanded. An examination of a contour map of Norway illustrates how difficult it was to move large numbers of troops and war materials from one point to another. There were only two land routes in North Norway:

▶ the railroad that had its northernmost terminal in Mo I Rana

▶ *Riksvei* 50 which, north of Trondheim, became a sea of mud in the spring when the frost went out and, due to heavy snow and narrow construction, was difficult to use in the winter

In order to survey the special problems presented by Norway and North Norway in particular, Hitler sent no less a person than General List to Norway in February, 1942. His report to Hitler maintained that it was essential to improve northern communications by lengthening *Riksvei* 50 to stretch all the way to Karasjok.[148] Also, a railway in North Norway (from Mo to Kirkenes) was to be given high priority and construction should start at the earliest possible time.[149] The work force to carry out these tasks was to be comprised of 5,000 Russian prisoners of war who were on their way to Norway. The Russians and other Eastern Europeans were used to construct the road over the Korgen Mountain *(Korgenfjell)* south of Mosjøen at such a loss of life that the road was called the Bloodway *(Blodvegen)*.

Not only did Hitler want transportation improved but he wanted air fields, bombproof submarine bases in Trondheim and Bergen and dry docks to accommodate the biggest German ships. Plans were to be prepared for increased aluminum and magnesium production.[150] Hitler would not be satisfied until Norway was "Fortress Norway," able to withstand any Allied attack.

## Norway was on Hitler's Mind in 1942

In the fall of 1942, Hitler had accomplished many of his aims in Norway. He had strengthened his position there so that it would have entailed great losses for the Allies to attempt a landing. On the other hand, Hitler had not forgotten the demands of the rest of occupied Europe, even though Norway was foremost on his mind during the first half of 1942.

It was on August 17, 1942, that the British mounted the last in the series of big raids that were carried out by combined operations in Norway (the systematic phase as we have called these big raids). If deception of the Germans was their aim, the British had accomplished their goal in Norway. In his fear of invasion through Norway, Hitler had strengthened his defenses there at the expense of other areas. In the fall of 1942 there were 40 German divisions in Europe to prevent an invasion from the west that did not come that year.[151] However, it was not in Norway, or even in Europe, that the Allied offensive came, but rather in North Africa on November 8, 1942, as Operation Torch. All plans of invasions in the Balkans, southern France, western France or in Norway were shelved. Even Churchill's pet, Jupiter, the operation to liberate North Norway, was shelved. In July 1942, Churchill had to give up his plan that with the "right claw" the Allies could carry out Torch (earlier called Gymnast) and with the left could implement Jupiter. "At every point except one the plans I had cherished were

■ **Resistance fighters keep in contact with each other from well-hidden places**

adopted. "Jupiter" alone I could not carry, although its merits were not disputed. I did not give up this plan yet, but in the end I failed to establish it."[152] With the inception of Torch, the Allies gave up plans to make Norway the second front in 1942.[153]

## 1942 – The Beginning of the End

The fall of 1942 marks the turning of the hinge of fate or "the beginning of the end" as it also has been called.[154] The Allies began their offensive on two fronts, the invasion of Africa and the breakthrough at Stalingrad. Despite El Alamein and Stalingrad, Hitler still felt that Norway was the danger zone in this war.[155] German troops were not drawn from Norway until 1943 when Hitler evidently became convinced that the greatest danger lay in the continental, not Scandinavian part of Europe.

If the British intent in 1941-42 was to confuse the Germans as to their real intentions with raids and other forms of sabotage, they succeeded. But they also confused someone else, their Norwegian allies.

To return to the Majavatn episode, when the agents who had been trained in England came to Vefsen *Herred* in late 1941 they went to the police office in Mosjøen and were given false identity papers by a Norwegian who was already in the illegal resistance work. This person was a relative of Erling Grannes. Then they went to a farm near Mosjøen owned by the father of one of the agents, Lynghaug. From there they moved to the Grannes farm at Tangen near Majavatn in February, 1942. Word circulated in the neighborhood that young Lynghaug had returned from England, and the presence of these agents became common knowledge. These young men brought with them weapons and ammunition, as mentioned before. Also, they had been told that an invasion was to come, certainly before September and most probably in August, 1942, after sufficient quantities of weapons had been accumulated.

The local Norwegians threw themselves wholeheartedly into the work. A man from Fellingfors (Magnus Paulssen) even used his truck to transport weapons along *Riksvei* 50. The Grannes farm became a virtual arsenal with weapons such as grenades and automatic rifles stored there. The weapons were secreted in the woods and around the buildings, and the resistance even stored 200-300 kilos of explosives under the house. At least a ton and a half of war materials were stored on the Grannes farm alone. The summer went by and more men and more supplies were brought into Vistenfjord, split up and dispersed over the area of Grane *Kommune*. There were, throughout the spring, at least three boat loads of weapons and several other boats that brought new men, so that in May/June there were, as Erling Grannes has said, close to 25 tons of weapons. By September 1942 at least 40 men had come to augment the original five who had come to Mosjøen in December.

People worked hard, but they also talked quite openly. It didn't matter much if the talk spread, or so many Norwegians thought, for the Germans would be pushed out in a short while. Many of the men who worked with the illegal transport of men and material wanted to know more than the next so the loose talk continued and rumors spread.

The British sent messages to the group stationed at Majavatn and they also expected reports since the activities were, in fact, ordered and led from England. There was no electricity on the Grannes farm so the telegraphist Reidar Årkvisla—alias Reidar Christiansen, made frequent trips into Trofors to attend to his radio. His trips soon caught the interest of the Gestapo, and it was not long before he was sought by the Germans for arrest. The remainder of the story has been related before in Chapter 1, on Majavatn.

In spite of all the contacts the resistance group had with the British, they had little contact with the nearest Milorg group that was just over the county border in Nord-Trøndelag. If there was little coordination of activities between Nordland *Fylke* and Nord-Trøndelag Fylke, there was even less between the British and Milorg in Norway in the year 1942. After the Germans picked up the trail of the group at Majavatn, they began an intensive campaign to clean up the resistance in the whole of Norway. Too many people knew too much and it became, as the Norwegian expression has it, a rolling-up.[156]

# Chapter 9

## *NASJONAL SAMLING'S* ATTEMPT TO LEAD NORWAY

**It was in this same year, 1942** that Quisling was named Minister President of Norway. We know that there was a great deal of soul-searching on this subject. Terboven had grave misgivings about the ability of Quisling to handle such an important position. Terboven had doubts that a Quisling government would find any genuine support among the Norwegian people. Therefore, a government led by Quisling would be only a shell needing constant German support. Consequently, such a government would be of no real value. Terboven was, however, willing to give Quisling the chance to prove himself. The reasons for this willingness are debatable. [157] However, it is known that Terboven was not present at the "enthronement" in Akershus on February 1, 1942.[158]

We have fairly good authority for stating that Terboven was playing a double role in the case of Quisling's desire for complete power (known as *Statsaken*). Gerhard Berghold *Ministerialrat of Reichskommissariat Norwegen,* claimed that Terboven was forced by Berlin to find a place for Quisling. On the other hand, Terboven was crafty enough to make it appear as though he, of his own free will, was finding the place for Quisling. It is Berghold's contention that Terboven was determined to carry Quisling to the heights and thereby show Hitler once and for all how useless Quisling was and would be. Terboven looked on with delight when Quisling made a fool of himself by persecuting school teachers and church ministers. Even though he knew it was a mistake, Terboven did nothing to stop it. The idea was to get Quisling out on thin ice and then let him sink. It is for this reason, Berghold maintained, that Terboven himself asked Hitler to make Quisling Minister President.[159]

It therefore appears that it was not the *Wehrmacht* that prevented Quisling from taking over the complete reins of government in February 1942, but rather the raids by the British, the work of the SOE, and the fear that the Allied push would come through Norway.

■ **The First Norwegian Battalion holds a parade in East Finnmark in 1945**

## World Press Reaction to Quisling as Head of State of Norway

After Quisling's installation as the head of state of Norway, the reaction in the world press was unfavorable. Goebbels was aware that Quisling had come to stand for evil in the world and that he was the prototype and his name was synonymous with traitor. Goebbels also believed that the more Quisling was attacked, the more the Germans would have to support him. As a result, he had an interesting reaction to the Quisling state visit to Berlin on February 12-15, 1942 during which Quisling hoped to receive a promise of a peace treaty and the right to independence, including the right to rebuild the Norwegian army and defenses. Goebbels characterized Quisling's desires in four words *"Das is naturlich naiv"* (that is naïve). Goebbels did say, however, that a dogmatic theorist such as Quisling could not be expected to have a really clear grasp of statecraft.[160]

Goebbels said once that one had to proceed with caution when the Nazification of a people was at stake. Quisling did not have the necessary degree of patience. As of February 1, 1942, he thought he had the power and believed it was time to use it against those who opposed him. Previously, he had said to the Norwegian people, "Either you shall follow us, or you shall be driven into the ground."[161] He also said, "All passiveness must be cleared away and all opposition must be beaten down. The Norwegian people shall move forward."[162] He had already demonstrated his willingness to use the iron hand with the publication of the so-called *jossinglister* (enemies' lists), which initiated the fight against the Home Front.[163]

Quisling did not have the politicians' practical eye for detecting public opinion. His predominant goal was to Nazify the Norwegian people in the shortest possible time. He did not have the political skill to work through devious routes that were often necessary to achieve his objectives. The forces that he called upon to move Norway along the road of Nazism were too weak to carry through, and Quisling did not have the power to bolster them when they faltered or failed. When he tried, through naked

■ **Norwegian ski patrols were adept at fighting the Nazis in mountainous terrain**

power, to smash resistance, it only served to strengthen that very resistance and to make it return with greater vigor. This was demonstrated early in the battle he waged against the Church (*kirkestriden*), against the teachers (*lærerstriden*), against the youth (*ungdomstjenesten*), the government (*rikstinget*), and the workers (*arbeidstjensten*). Likewise, his ineffectiveness was demonstrated through his attempted reorganization of the basic township government of Norway (*kommuneforvaltningen*) and many other of his cherished "New Order" ideals.[164]

The situation became so grave that on August 11, 1942, the Fuhrer himself called a meeting that included *Reichsaussenminister* (Foreign Minister) von Ribbentrop, *der Reichminister und Chef der Reichskanslei* (Cabinet Minister and Chief of the Church), Dr. Lanners, *der Reichsleiter* (Nazi Party leader) Martin Borman, and *der Reichskommissar* (State Commission for Norway) Terboven. Hitler was enraged over the situation in Norway. He had expected peace and order in Norway. After all, they were fellow Nordics. But instead, opposition in Norway was greater than ever. One must remember this was less than one month before the Majavatn episode. Hitler feared an Allied invasion and Quisling had helped to create a strong resistance by his heavy-handed methods, exactly the thing Hitler had wished to avoid. Hitler ordered that Quisling should cease all talk of a peace treaty with Germany and as long as the war lasted, the relative positions of Norway and Germany would remain unchanged. He also ordered that Quisling should do nothing without Terboven's authorization. One can imagine Terboven's feeling on hearing this, as he had planned for just this eventuality and was able to place all the blame for the strengthened resistance on Quisling.[165] Quisling remained what he had always been, a tool for the oppression of his own people.

Quisling was reduced to Terboven's puppet. For Quisling this was a hard blow. He clearly understood how weak he really was at the close of the important year 1942. In 1943, as he talked to some of Terboven's men, he said, "German Nazism is nothing more than camouflage for the worst kind of imperialism; it oppresses its own allies with naked power. Had I known how I would be treated, I would have acted differently the 9th of April 1940. The new Europe will be born, but against Germany."[166]

The era of Quisling can be best summed up in words he himself wrote during the fight with the Church: "It is the people's curse that small men in high positions without foresight and historical perspective, for selfish gains, ruin that which is created by intelligent and nationalistically-minded men through generations of work and then cannot see the long lasting and great damage they do."[167] With these words Quisling wrote his own epitaph.

# Chapter 10

## MILORG AND SOE MOVE CLOSER TOGETHER

**As of January 1, 1942,** the British SOE established a separate branch to deal only with the resistance movement in Norway. As the chief of the Norwegian Section SOE, *Oberst Løytnant* J. S. Wilson was placed under the direction of Sir Charles Hambro in the Ministry of Economic Warfare. From February 6, 1942, the Norwegian government established the *Forsvarets Overkommando* (FO) under General Wilhelm Hansteen who in turn reported to Oskar Torp in the Defense Ministry. FO was to coordinate and command all three Norwegian military branches.[168] On February 16, 1942, representatives of SOE and FO met for the first time and formed a committee for joint prosecution of the war. This committee was named the Anglo-Norwegian Collaboration Committee (ANCC) and it became the highest authority for decisions on military resistance policy regarding Norway.[169] Even though the committee was established easily in London, it was to prove more difficult and take longer to establish close cooperation down through the ranks, between SOE and MI IV in Stockholm and between Milorg and SOE in Norway.[170]

It was about time that the British and Norwegians began to work cooperatively in the resistance. The preceding chapters have shown how challenging 1942 proved to be. In more than one way, 1942 was perhaps the most interesting year of the military resistance in Norway. Among the factors contributing to the challenge were the British raids, the German fear of invasion, the *Nasjonal Samling's* push for Nazification, the Statsak and Quisling, the increasing resistance of the Norwegian people, the tremendous drive by the Nazis to crush opposition, as evidenced by the arrests and terror of 1942. The mass arrests of late 1942 showed how weak the resistance was and that all concerned had underestimated the strength of the Germans and their desire to be rid of the resistance movement. However hard-hit the resistance (both SOE and Milorg) was, some good did come of the situation. It became clear that there was a primary need for a unified military resistance organization under unified leadership, with common goals and methods.

As has been mentioned, several times in 1941 and early 1942 the British intimated that there would perhaps be a landing in Norway sometime in 1942. This, as has been seen, led to a considerable amount of loose talk in Norway with consequences that should have been, but were not, anticipated. This was the case at Majavatn. Secondly, from the British standpoint there were questions as to the worth of the Norwegian resistance in any planned military action. It was these very questions, and the possibility of invasion, that led to discussions about the secret home resistance.

■ **A German military vehicle flies a white flag of surrender in 1945**

On January 19, 1942, the Milorg leadership delivered its position at a meeting with SOE. It was declared that Milorg would be of vital importance in any anticipated action in Norway. It was further declared that it should be Norwegian leadership that would decide the type of activity in which Milorg should participate.[171] Milorg further wanted to delay any military action on its part until such time as a permanent reconquest of all of Norway was begun. This plan, of course, could not be fully accepted by SOE as it would seriously disturb plans for short-term activities such as Churchill's idea to cut Norway in half: to free Northern Norway.

Milorg wanted to settle the problems concerning all possible plans of action. How was Milorg to act in any given circumstance, i.e., all-out invasion, partial invasion, beachhead invasion, or a faltering invasion? There were a multitude of possibilities and Milorg wanted the blueprint of a plan of action. SOE answered this by saying it would be impossible to bind themselves so tightly and not allow flexibility of operation. Further, everything must be sent at zero hour from Great Britain to prevent premature disclosure.[172]

There also had to be some agreement between Milorg and SOE as to the role to be played by strikes against communication, transportation, and manufacturing in Norway. There had to be coordination so that local groups of SOE and Milorg did not stumble over each other.

At the same time the Norwegian government was also anxious to see some accommodation reached. This was true because it feared that if it could not control the home resistance forces and assure the British of the loyalty of the resistance, the British might potentially work outside of the Norwegian Defense Ministry and thereby undermine Norwegian authority.

To establish cooperation, a meeting was held in Stockholm on February 6-17, 1942. From the Norwegian Army Command *(Hærens Overkommando)* came John Rognes, and from Milorg came L. D. Rolstad. These two men agreed in principle that Milorg would only go into full-scale action if it appeared that a general invasion would be successful. They also agreed that only some sections of Milorg would take action if certain districts were invaded, and that the rest of Milorg would remain passive so as to retain its secrecy.[173] This was reported back to London and met with the approval of both FO and SOE. The Anglo-Norwegian Collaboration Committee was now working as was intended. The visit by John Rognes to Stockholm had also helped to smooth relations between Milorg and British representatives there.[174] However, the cooperation newly found in Stockholm still did not immediately extend to Norway. Relations continued to be strained throughout 1942. There continued to be parallel lines of action in many parts of the country.

In Southern Norway the SOE operative "Biscuit" came to organize military resistance in an area where Central Leadership (SL) of Milorg already had a man working. Many bitter words were exchanged between "Biscuit," his predecessor (Cheese) Odd Starheim, and the Milorg leader Arne Laudel.[175] In yet another example "Anvil" came to the Lillehammer district. He was suspected by Milorg of being an agent provocateur and was nearly shot as such. "Anvil" was to work to build up a group under SOE in absolute secrecy, outside of Milorg. This proved to be impossible in such a small area as Lillehammer.[176] There is little wonder that Milorg had reason to suspect the activities and motives of strangers in their midst.

In the Majavatn area there was only one contact person between the men who came to the Grannes farm at Majavatn in Nordland and the Milorg group only a few miles south at Smalåsen in Nord-Trøndelag. Vidar Smalås was this contact man. Vidar Smalås had direct orders from his superior, Nissen Meyer, to withhold information from the men from England and to keep his ears open for any information valuable to Milorg. The suspicion was great enough on the part of Milorg in the late summer of 1942 to suspend any further activity because of the open activity of the SOE agents at Majavatn. When the crash came in September, 1942, the caution of Milorg had paid off; only Vidar Smalås of Milorg was arrested. He stated in a report dated August 8, 1946, that, "The grounds for my arrest, I presume, were that one of the men from Grane (Majavatn) had talked under torture, however he had no other knowledge of our organization than that I was the contact man. No other members of our organization were arrested at that time."[177]

Fortunately, the problems that presented themselves to SOE-Milorg cooperation were not insurmountable. Part of the blame for the serious consequences at Majavatn and other places where SOE agents were captured or thwarted could be ascribed to the fact that most of these agents, as had been the case at Majavatn, were there on short term assignments. The thinking was that "the invasion comes tomorrow, so who needs to be cautious?" Also the natural Norwegian tendency to trust old friends and relatives and to sometimes talk too much at the wrong time can be blamed. The resistance also under-estimated

**The Supreme Headquarters of Allied Expedition Forces announces Quisling's arrest**

the enemy's counter espionage, the Nazi willingness to "play in the negative sector." Further, the many months of successful, undisturbed work had encouraged a feeling of security. The men from England came to the Majavatn area in January 1942 and worked nearly the entire year before the "rolling-up" in September. Too many knew too much. Men worked both for SOE and Milorg and thereby increased their knowledge of other resistance people and also increased the risk of being caught. This was one of the dangers in the aforementioned incident in South Norway and at Lillehammar. This was the very thing Nissen Meyer sought to avoid between Nord-Trøndelag and Nordland.

## Solution to Resistance Problems: The Norwegian People at Home

The solution was to use the people at home in Norway, people who knew the latest rules and regulations instituted by the Germans, to organize a system whereby each man knew only one other so as to reduce chances of such mass arrests as occurred in Smalåsen. Resistance members were instructed that if the man on either side of you was arrested, you were to go into hiding so as to break the chain of knowledge. Watertight cells of activity were constructed and the series of cut-outs were instituted. Further, it was decided that SOE would be primarily a specialist force to train local Milorg groups in the use of espionage equipment and weapons. These specialists would be sent only when Milorg asked for them and was prepared to give them cover. SOE, following its new policy of late 1942, also agreed that the new agents should be trained with the *Kompani Linge* men, that their final instructions should be given by officers of both SOE and the Norwegian Defense Command (FO), and that the orders needed to be approved by the Norwegian Defense Minister. SOE would provide the transportation and supplies but from that time on the SOE operatives were told to stay in contact with the entire Home Front leadership, including Milorg.

The word went out, after the staggering blows in the fall of 1942, for cooperation on the part of SOE with the Home Front along all lines. The resistance in Norway came under one leadership and came to have one view of the military resistance in occupied Norway. At the beginning of 1943, then, it could be said that the resistance was over the top and had gained in experience, in strength, and possibly in wisdom.[178]

# Chapter 11

# IN THE SHADOW OF THE GREAT WAR

**In 1943, one began to feel that the initiative** of the war was now on the side of the Allies. They launched operations against El Alamein in French North West Africa. They also broke the Russians out of Stalingrad after a long siege. Each month showed more clearly that the Allies were no longer the underdogs in the war.[179] This was illustrated first and most strongly in Trenis, when the last Germans on Cape Bon Peninsula capitulated May 13, 1943. It was clear that before long Sicily and Italy would be invaded. From Sicily and Italy the Allies would "roll up the map of Europe."[180]

As discussed earlier, Hitler believed Norway to be the area where the Allies would invade Europe. Even in 1943, in April, Hitler wanted to send two divisions to Norway, "in addition to the normal."[181] Why did Hitler still feel that Norway would present the danger? Magne Skodvin, in *Historisk Tidsskrift*, 1951, feels there were two reasons. First, the invasion of Europe would have to come on both military and political grounds. It was uncertain whether the English would want to fight a war on a wide front in Europe, while it was certain that the Allies would want good bases in Europe. If these two conditions were the case, then one could reasonably expect the Allies to invade through Norway, for it was here that the German troops were most insecure because of supply problems. Second, the western powers would wish to take Norway in order to keep the Russians out.[182] Hitler felt that the invasion would come in the spring of 1944 through Norway. To prepare for this major onslaught, at least sixty to eighty submarines were to be concentrated in Norwegian waters. Hitler, however, said that the Air Force and Army would have to make do with what they already had. In this connection, General Jodl reported that there now were approximately 430,000 men in Norway, but that there had been more. Hitler remarked that this was a colossal number and equaled the peace time strength of the entire French Army.

■ **Crown Prince Olav rides in a victory parade, greeting the people of Norway in 1945**

Hitler felt that 430,000 men and sixty to eighty submarines, along with coastal artillery were not enough, when the *Scharnhorst* was lost in December 1943, and he considered sending the *Prinz Eugen* northward. It was vital to keep the north coast in German hands "because it hinders the British invasion plans, and has also something to say about the situation in the Pacific."[183]

In January and February of 1944 a meeting was held in Moscow to plan Operation Body Guard, a camouflage for the invasion. This Bodyguard was to make Hitler think the invasion of Europe would come through Scandinavia and the Mediterranean, before the attack really came from both East and West.[184] In Bodyguard the Allies created a plan that mirrored what Hitler had felt all along. Nearly a half million men with arms were positioned in Norway awaiting an attack that would never come, despite the fact that there was a grave need for them elsewhere.[185] Hitler had increased his manpower in Norway from 13 divisions (380,000 men) on November 7, 1943, to 430,000 men on December 20 of the same year.[186]

About a week after the sinking of the Scharnhorst at Nordkapp, Doenitz and Hitler agreed to send the *Prinz Eugen* to North Norway, "because that will work against British invasion plans."[187]

This Plan Bodyguard was personally inspired by Churchill. He had committed himself strongly to Operation Jupiter in 1942-43 to relieve the Russians and free North Norway. He had backed off from that plan, but, his interest in an invasion of North Norway was not dead. On February 19, 1944, he wrote to General Ismay "I do not think it wise to rule out "Jupiter" finally from the operations of this war. We ought, of course, to have liberated Norway during the campaign of 1943, but our American allies would probably not have consented to such strategy and it would not have been possible to obtain the necessary support here." He also mentioned that if Overlord, the invasion in Europe, failed, it would perhaps be necessary to initiate flanking movements both in Norway and from Turkey and the Aegean at a later date.[188]

However much preparation the Germans made in Norway against an eventual invasion there, they could not lose sight of the fact that a push toward Germany's heart would have to come on the continent. After June 6, 1944 (D-Day), it was clear that Overlord was in operation and that Bodyguard and Norway were to remain in the shadow of the great war in Europe.

Despite Norway being in the shadow of the Great War, the Allied desire to damage the German war potential wherever they could remained unchanged. Even if the plans for Jupiter and Bodyguard were placed on the shelf, the Allies believed that strategic bombing should be carried out in Norway. This was opposed by the Norwegian government in London who, while they were in favor of defeating the enemy, were hesitant to approve methods of warfare that would lead to the destruction of Norwegian life and property. There was, however, a tactic other than bombing, namely sabotage. In this matter the Norwegian officials in London received support from the Home Front in Norway.[189] In 1943 and throughout 1944, the feeling grew that the most effective warfare in Norway would be through sabotage. In 1943-1944 extensive sabotage was carried out by SOE and Milorg agents against shipping, industry, and railroads.

## Naval Sabotage

Sabotage of German ships was carried out in many different ways. One method of sabotage was to fasten magnetic mines to the hulls of German ships. However, this form of sabotage did not achieve the desired results: the sinking of German ships in Norwegian harbors. Other forms of sabotage were tried, i.e., small one man u-boats and "chariots." A chariot was a self-propelled torpedo designed to be hung on the outside of a small boat and then directed at the target.[190]

## Industrial Sabotage

In this type of sabotage the SOE and Milorg were more successful, and the most successful action of all was the destruction of the heavy-water plant at Rjukan in Telemark. Nine men from *Kompani Linge*, code-named "Gunnerside-Swallow," planted explosives

■ The city of Oslo celebrates the liberation of Norway with massive fireworks

in the only heavy water plant of any consequence in Europe, the Norsk Hydro Plant at Rjukan in Telemark. The explosion in the early morning of March 28, 1943 was an explosion that the War Cabinet in London and the SOE had awaited for a long time. Until after the war when the atomic age came to light, the results and the importance of this act of sabotage were known only to those directly concerned with production of radioactive materials. The Germans reacted strongly to this act of sabotage and about one hundred people in and around Rjukan were arrested. The result was that many people active in Milorg and other phases of the resistance had to flee the country.[191]

This successful act of sabotage was not successful in defeating the Nazi war machine. The damage was repaired and production resumed. On November 16, 1943, the plant at Rjukan was bombed without serious results except the loss of 21 Norwegian lives. On the 30th of November it was learned that the Germans were going to dismantle the heavy water plant and ship it to Germany. The materials would be shipped out over Lake Tinnsjø. The Germans reinforced the guard in the area; however, for some unexplained reason, they failed to guard the rail ferry over Lake Tinnsjø. This made it possible for Knut Haukelid of Operation Gunnerside, Knut Lier-Hansen of Milorg and Rolf Sorlie of the Rjukan underground to sneak aboard the ferry on the night of February 19, 1944 and plant explosives. The ferry sank the next forenoon on Tinnsjø. This ended the battle for heavy water; the Germans did not produce more heavy water in Norway.[192]

Many sabotage actions were carried out through the cooperation of SOE and Milorg. Among these actions were the sabotage of the Stapo quarters in Haugusbygd, a *Luftwaffe* depot in Tønsberg, and the machine shop at the Kongsberg weapons factory.[193]

## Railway Sabotage

In the case of railway sabotage the action of both the SOE and the resistance had a long history. Late in the war railway sabotage was an important goal for the Norwegians, intended to hinder the rapid movement of German troops from Norway to other points in continental Europe to enhance the defense of Germany itself. The climax of these actions came on the night of March 14, 1945, when the north-south railroads in Norway were cut in a thousand different places at the same time.[194]

These glimpses of sabotage illustrate that Norway was in the shadow of the Great War. The Allied leadership did not want to tie down their troops in Norway, and their first solution was to try strategic bombing. However, Milorg and the SOE came to an agreement that sabotage could do the job just as effectively and with less cost in lives and property.

The acts of sabotage did not go unpunished by the Germans. Milorg men were arrested over all of Norway. On August 16, 1943, about 1,100 Norwegians, former military officers, were arrested in what Terboven hoped would be a crushing blow to Milorg.[195] This, however, was not the case, for while many of the leaders of Milorg were former officers, they had long since trained civilians to assume their Milorg duties in the event of just such an action on the part of the Germans.[196] The period of 1943 and the first half of 1944 was a period of hard times for the resistance, similar to the fall of 1942, but it did not signal a diminishing of the resistance. Rather, the hard times strengthened the resistance and made it more cautious.

# Chapter 12

## THE ROLE OF MILORG
## BEFORE AND DURING THE LIBERATION

**The end of 1942 and the new year of 1943** made it clear that the war had passed a turning point. In connection with this new situation the overall strategy of the Allies was opened to discussion. The Allied policy toward Norway was also considered for revision. One result of this was that a new direction was defined for Milorg's work before and during the anticipated liberation. There was opposition to overcome, several misunderstandings to be resolved between the British and the Norwegians, as well as misunderstanding between Norwegians both outside and within Norway. Misunderstandings between the civil home leadership *(Sivilorg)* and the military home leadership, Milorg, had to be resolved. Again, revisions had to be considered with the progress of 1943 into 1944. Discussions centered on the roles that various actions would play in the coming liberation.

In the case of Majavatn, and in many other cases, the military resistance had been hard hit by German reprisals in 1942. In most cases these had followed the discovery of some SOE group or some action that had been sponsored by the SOE. The British in the SOE maintained that their work was necessary to make Norway "a thorn in the German side." The war was a total war and the Norwegians on the Home Front had to bear their share of the entire Allied burden. The Norwegians in the Defense High Command (FO) also felt this to be the case, but they were not in complete agreement with all of the British plans.[197] However, SOE and FO agreed that the work in Norway must continue, reprisals or not. This was the feeling then of those directing activities from outside Norway. But what of the views of those closest to the actual scene?

The civil resistance early in 1942 had taken a hands-off attitude toward active warfare on the Home Front. The catalyst to harden this policy was a bomb attack on the *Statspolitets* headquarters at Henrik Ibsensgate in Oslo, by a Communist-led group. The civil resistance leader, "Jenny" wrote to Foreign Minister Trygve Lie and said that further activities of this kind would most certainly lead to heavy reprisals and the shooting of hostages by the Germans. He also said that he knew "with certainty" that a Russian officer had recently been in Norway with instructions for Communist-led groups. "Jenny" pleaded with Lie to stop any further actions of this kind through whatever diplomatic channels were at his disposal. Finally, "Jenny" said, "A tactic which can be used in Serbia is not acceptable for Norway, where the circumstances are different. Our allies can be assured that when we have elected to follow a line of passive resistance, it is not because we are not willing to sacrifice, for innumerable Norwegians are ready to offer their lives for freedom, but rather it is because it is the only reasonable form of battle against Nazism and Germany for us today."[198]

The military home leadership did not so categorically declare itself, but from early fall of 1942 it did not engage in quite such active warfare as had been the case before.

The questions of strategies and leadership of the resistance were of grave concern throughout the fall of 1942, not least because of the Majavatn affair. Also, there was little real contact between the civil and military arms of the resistance. The leaders of each of these two groups were not even certain about who were the leaders of other groups, and it was not until meetings in November and December of 1942 in Stockholm that a great deal of misunderstanding was cleared up. Representatives of the two resistance groups met with a representative of FO.[199] These conferences were necessary because Milorg showed *Sivilorg* that it was not responsible for the events from Telavåg to Majavatn. It also assured Sivilorg that Milorg was not in favor of the kind of active strategy advocated by SOE. Finally, Milorg assured Sivilorg that the leadership of Milorg *(Rådet-R)* did not desire to be solely responsible for directing resistance in Norway at the expense of the leaders of the civil resistance.[200]

## Need for Agreement Between Milorg and Norwegian Government in London

There needed to be some agreement between Milorg and the Norwegian government in London under Prime Minister Nygaardsvold. Milorg viewed the war in Norway from three different scenarios, (1) Allied invasion without the help of Milorg, (2) Allied invasion with limited Milorg action, (3) Allied invasion with action of Milorg in all districts. Rådet believed that if Milorg were to be effective four conditions had to be met:

▶ Milorg had to be intact.
▶ Milorg had to have necessary supplies, weapons, ammunition, explosives, communications equipment, and food.
▶ FO had to inform Milorg in advance of objectives in each district.
▶ FO had to give Milorg advance notice of the planned invasion.[201]

■ King Haakon and Crown Prince Olav salute the celebrating crowds on their way to Akershus Fortress

FO was not ready at this time, April, 1943, to answer in the affirmative to the four conditions advanced by Milorg. FO held to the idea that the liberation of Norway had to be an integral part of the entire Allied wartime strategy. FO could not promise to send the requested information on any planned invasion, but it would send instructors and instruction material to be used by Milorg in preparation for action. However, as a new condition, FO stated that all Milorg actions would have to be cleared with London. Prior to this Milorg had the right to act on its own

■ **King Haakon presides over the opening session of the newly- formed Storting (parliament).**

initiative by initiating appropriate action throughout the districts in the event of an invasion. This new condition was a great disappointment to Milorg, and it requested a meeting with FO. The meeting was held May 7-9, 1943 in Køpmannabro in Värmland, Sweden. Representing FO in London, *Oberstløytnant* Bjarne Øen and Captain Jakob Schive, for FO affiliate in Stockholm, *Oberst* Ole Berg and for *Rådet* Major Olaf Helset and Jens Christian Hauge, Dr. Carl Semb and Lieutenant Lasse Heyerdahl Larsen.[202] These men represented the most thorough knowledge of Milorg and the military situation both on the Home Front and outside of Norway.

The protocol agreed upon at this meeting is one of the most important documents of the resistance history.

# Translation of the Protocol in Brief

Representatives for *Forsvarets Overkommando* (FO) and *Militær organisasjonens Rådet* (R) are after conferences in May, 1943 in agreement on the following protocol, which is presented to FO and R for approval.

(1) That Norwegian youth should be trained in the use of modern weapons, with thought both to a home force during an invasion and to establish new groups at home in the future. This training gives youth a practical assignment in the waiting period that bolsters patriotism and supports the Norwegian government in England.

(2) *Forsvarets Overkommando* has final authority if and to what degree forces of Milorg shall be used during an invasion to support the invasion within the country. Milorg relinquishes the right to independent action in the event of an invasion. *Rådet* will maintain a strong discipline to prevent uncontrolled action by its ranks. It is recognized that there are groups outside of Milorg not controlled by Milorg which are active resistance units. To prevent patriotic youth from joining these organizations, it is necessary that Norwegian officials support Milorg, which stands on constitutional ground.

(3) An eventual uprising of Milorg can come either through the command apparatus or another organ that FO finds it necessary to use. R is willing to cooperate with another organ whose use is necessary. The method of such cooperation is thus:
   a. Milorg's central and district administration are to remain intact. Expansion of radio connection with FO continues with the goal that all districts get direct connection.
   b. Any new organization that FO may use must not establish a district administration outside of Milorg.
   c. FO will continue to send instructors and materials to instruct all districts in the use of modern weapons and explosives.
   d. FO will continue to help the home districts in choice of goals.
   e. Success of an uprising through any other organization, than the district administration, must be certain.

(4) R realizes that FO has connections to groups not now under Milorg and that there can be requests for FO to organize like groups in other districts. It is hoped—especially with the thought that the Germans may evacuate without an invasion—that these groups be bound to Milorg.

(5) R realizes that FO will carry out operations in the interim before an invasion and it may be necessary for secrecy. These operations may be out without the help of Milorg.

(6) The military inspector in Stockholm represents FO in its work in Norway. Any direct contact between him and the districts must not lead to districts coming into direct contact with each other. SL coordinates and administers the work in the districts.

■ **A Norwegian sailor poses in front of a cartoon of the lion, Norway's symbol, sinking a German submarine.**

In the districts to which he does not have direct communication, the military inspector will be given contacts to be used in emergency.

(7) To preclude the Allies from taking over civil administration in a greater degree than is necessary—either with occupation after battle, or after German withdrawal without battle—it is necessary that secret civilian administration apparatus be built in loyal cooperation with the government. This administration will stand ready to step in with Allied military officials when the moment comes. Such an administration is necessary in the interval between German withdrawal and the return of our constitutional government.

It is also desirable that the government and FO on their part, inform those who work in Norway of their thoughts on the above situation.[203]

## Milorg Was Not Opposed to Outlines of Protocol

Milorg was not opposed to a division of responsibilities such as was outlined by the protocol. Quite the opposite was true. Milorg had, from the start, believed that the officials in London should take the leadership and had stated so in a letter to King

Haakon on June 10, 1941. However, it was necessary for all concerned to meet and re-affirm that Milorg was loyal to the government.[204] In June, 1943, Nygaardsvold wrote home and said, "Milorg should not be concerned with other than purely military and military assistance organizations."[205]

Point 7 did create some discussion between the government and *Sivilorg*. *Sivilorg* believed it would be a direct insult to Norwegians to have German occupation supplanted by Allied occupation. However, these bitter feelings were somewhat assuaged by reassurance from London that Allied administration would only be necessary to insure a successful reconquest. However, *Sivilorg* would not graciously accept this fact and continued to be skeptical of Allied plans. This is illustrated by the letter of the Minister of Justice Terje Wold, to the Home Front, and by the voluminous correspondence between *Sivilorg* and the government.[206]

The meeting of May 7-9, 1943, clarified the role of Milorg during a potential invasion but did not outline a plan for the possibility of a German evacuation or German capitulation. Rådet took up these eventualities with *Sivilorg* and *Polorg*. After these discussions, Jens Christian Hauge authored a letter that *Rådet* sent to FO On August 31, 1943.

*Rådet* expressed a desire to prevent chaos in the period between German capitulation-evacuation and the arrival of Allied troops. This lead to a weakness of Milorg in North Norway, and Milorg was at that time somewhat under strength in the South, West and in Trøndelag.[207]

The problems related to German capitulation-evacuation were extensive. How was Milorg to prevent individual activists from sniping at the retreating enemy? And even though the Milorg groups were not to engage in unapproved action, they had orders to disrupt any German attempt to destroy Norwegian property. Also, the question of the Quislings (traitors) needed to be considered. The letter recommended that, to preclude any possibility of civil war, Milorg would have to disarm and take into custody Quislings, and that the FO would have to send, as quickly as possible, airborne troops to assist Milorg. An alternative possibility was that the Germans would neither capitulate nor evacuate, but that command would break down. Norway could face a long and drawn-out war against last ditch holdouts. There was the possibility that German Nazis would be joined by Norwegian Quislings. In such an event, Milorg would be hard pressed to prevent a general vigilante action against the Quislings.[208]

Milorg decided that German capitulation was the most likely scenario and that all Nazis and Quislings must, at that moment be rendered harmless. There were still some points of difference between the civilian and the military Home Front to be ironed out. *Rådet* wanted the leaders of the civil organization to go to a meeting in Stockholm, at which there would be representatives of the Norwegian government.

However, *Sivilorg* did not want to go. A meeting was held in October, 1943. The leaders of *Politiorganisasjonen* in Norway, Sven Arntzen and Milorg's Jens Christian Hauge met with the Minister of Justice Terje Wold and Andreae Aulie who had come from London. Ole Berg of FO was also there.[209]

At this meeting special consideration was given to the problem of reducing danger to the civilian population in Norway in case of either German capitulation or evacuation. There had to be a special effort to inform the general populace of the possibility of German reprisals and other dangers.

## Joint Declaration to Prime Minister, 1943

A result of this meeting was the joint declaration to the Prime Minister of November 15, 1943. This letter was approved by *Rådet* of Milorg, *Politiorganisasjonen* leadership, and Kretsen of Sivilorg. The letter began with an attack upon the Communists because of their agitation for active warfare and their action in that direction, for example, their attack upon a German troop train in Mjøndalen on October 7, 1943. The letter went on to state that the main purpose of Milorg was to shape a military force in cooperation with the FO that the leadership outside of Norway could use as a force to support any plans for a retaking of Norway. Further, it was said that responsible military leaders outside of Norway must decide when, and to what degree the home forces shall be used after a careful consideration of the chances of success or failure of Allied plans for Norway.[210]

Once more, the letter pointed out the ever-present danger to the civilian population as a result of irresponsible activities against the Germans. The leadership of the Home Front reminded those outside Norway of the reprisals after the Allied bombing of Victoria Terrasse (police headquarters for the Germans in Norway), and Herøya and the actions in Telavåg and Majavatn. The Home Front maintained that an active warfare with armed attempts against Germans would only lead to more reprisals that, it was feared, might break the spirit of many Norwegians.

The Home Front further suggested in this letter that "our officials, in foreign countries, can best work against the activist line by enabling Milorg to instruct its members in the use of modern weapons. The provision of instruction material will enable our responsible military organization to better compete with those who seek a more active line against the enemy."[211]

This joint letter by the Home Front leadership was of utmost importance. It informed all involved that there was no longer any serious disagreement among the groups in Norway, who were in contact with the official government in London, as to the proper course of action in the period prior to the invasion. The letter further showed that the three main groups in the Home Front now were as one insofar as the proposed action of Milorg. The letter clearly represented the new unity that now prevailed on the Homefront.

**SOE and Milorg worked together in destroying the heavy-water plant at Rjukan in Telemark**

## SHAEF Director Outlining Allied Plans for Norway

In early 1944, SHAEF (Supreme Headquarters of Allied Expeditionary Forces) set forth directives outlining the Allied plans for Norway and for the proposed part that the home forces would play in these plans. SHAEF wanted to have several alternative plans for Norway but did not wish to put them into immediate action. This can be explained in part by the Allied concern for the proposed landings in France, Operation Overlord. SHAEF feared that action by home forces could lead to a general uprising that would need help from outside which SHAEF could not and would not be able to provide. SHAEF wanted to prevent a situation such as the one that had arisen in central France, which had caused a great deal of bitterness and criticism to come from French sources directed against the Allies. A similar situation in Norway could not, in SHAEF's opinion, be allowed. Therefore, SHAEF did not want to make any definite commitments and directed the home forces to avoid creating unrest in the population.[212] The home forces were to build and wait. They should prepare themselves to step in, in the event of German capitulation or evacuation in Norway. Their main objectives would be to (1) safeguard power stations, communications, industries, etc. against sabotage and destruction, and (2) to maintain peace and order.[213]

FO and *Rådet* were united in this view of the work to be done in Norway. To once more discuss the task of the Home Front, a meeting of FO and *Rådet* was held in Stockholm, March 14-28, 1944. This meeting discussed plans for work to be done in all the possible eventualities that would accompany the war's ultimate end, the unfinished organizational work in North Norway and the role of other organizations (gun clubs, workers' organizations, etc.) that could be called upon to help in any of the probable situations which could develop.[214]

In the case of German capitulation, the meeting underlined the importance of the police troops in Sweden, that these should be sent into Norway as soon as possible after an armistice had been declared. As to evacuation, great weight was placed on safeguarding Norwegian life and property. If necessary, it was felt that Milorg should fight with rearguard troops of the German army to preserve life and property. Also, steps to prevent the taking of Norwegian hostages by the Germans were emphasized. As to Allied invasion and German resistance, the parties agreed that the police and Milorg should function as interim police. They should serve as military police in the liberated areas under the command of the District Command (*Distrikts Kommando*), the East (DK Ø) South (DK S) West (DK V) Trøndelag (DK T) and North Norway (DK N).[215] In the main, this meeting reaffirmed the position taken by the various groups in August, 1943. The only serious variation was in the event of German evacuation with Milorg doing battle with the rearguard of the enemy. However, this was seen to be necessary, so it was now the official policy.

This Stockholm meeting took on increased importance in that the civil leadership also supported the conclusions. The Home Front organizations stood together with the same goals in mind.

On April 12, 1944, a "Proclamation from the Norwegian Home Front's Leadership," was read over the BBC from London and received support from the Norwegian government. This proclamation has been called the Home Front's "Magna Carta."[216]

The Norwegian Home Front's leadership, in cooperation with the king and government, represented a free and fighting Norway and made the following proclamation:

[We do not wish to enter into an international argument over boundaries, war crimes, aggressors, and reparations, etc. We want to deal only with Norwegian problems. These are the main points of our concern:

(1) A free, independent Norway.

(2) An immediate restoration of democracy.

(3) Revocation of laws either in the German interest or forced upon Norwegians by Germans or the NS.

(4) Immediate release of political prisoners and restoration of legal authorities.

(5) NS members who had harmed the state shall be punished, and illegal war profits shall be confiscated.

(6) A policy designed to
  a. safeguard freedom and democracy,
  b. restore the Norwegian economy, make use of natural resources and provide full employment.
  c. further the solidarity between classes and groups in society,
  d. work for international understanding, law and trade so as to shape a lasting peace.

If these goals are to be reached it is the duty of everyone to do his part, Norwegians, both at home and abroad, and our allies.

The battle is here at home, the same as on the front. Each of us is a soldier, civilian or in uniform. We are at war.

Cooperation and discipline are more necessary than ever. Follow those instructions and signals that are sent.]

The government in London, on the same day as the proclamation was read over the BBC, announced its full agreement with the principles outlined in the proclamation.[217]

This new-found cooperation between the leadership of the Home Front and the government was underlined when shortly thereafter Crown Prince Olav was named as Defense Chief for the entire Norwegian military effort. The reason for this appointment was to gain an absolute unity between the two fighting units of Norwegians, those at home and those abroad, so that the Home Front and the home forces could be used in SHAEF's plans for Norway.

Another sign of the improving relations was the establishment of the Special Forces headquarters on May 1, 1944. This led to more close-knit cooperation in the day-to-day work of FO, the SOE and the OSS. This led to the amalgamation of SOE, Norwegian Sector under J.S. Wilson and FO IV under Major Leif Tronstad which also improved cooperation.

## SHAEF and D-Day: New and Intense Efforts to Defeat the Nazis

When Operation Overlord was begun on June 6, 1944, the work of the Norwegian and Allied authorities took on a definite shape. The Norwegian home forces were an official part of the Allied forces and were under the command of SHAEF. It was SHAEF which in June, 1944, issued the following directive, entitled RESISTANCE IN NORWAY and read as follows:

■ **King Haakon VII, with the royal family in the background, accepts the salutes of Royal Norwegian Navy officers.**

(1) No Allied military offensive operations are planned for this theatre; therefore no steps must be taken to encourage the resistance movement as such to overt action, since no outside support can be forthcoming.

(2) It is appreciated that the situation in Norway will develop along one of the following lines given in order of probability:

    a. arising out of the collapse of Central Authority either in Germany or NORWAY or both following possibly on an unconditional surrender, a confused situation, rendering difficult to impossible the fulfillment of Armistice conditions;

    b. evacuation of the country North of Trondheim;

    c. complete evacuation of the country by the Germans.

(3) The activities of the resistance should be directed along the following lines:

    a. In any of the alternatives above-mentioned, the primary task is prevention of enemy execution of scorched earth policy. Protection should be afforded to targets in the following order of priority.

        i. Power stations.

        ii. Communications.

        iii. Public utilities (with special reference to ports and harbor installations).

b. In the event of a situation as 2a above, resistance groups should cooperate with the Civil Home Front organization for the purpose of maintaining law and order pending the arrival of an Allied relieving force;

c. Action on a limited scale may be called upon to prevent or hinder an evacuation. This must be undertaken by specialist groups, and in such a way as not to commit the movement as a whole, whose primary role, as stated in 3a is PROTECTIVE. Such action must not be undertaken except on orders from UK;

d. Current sabotage operations against enemy shipping and targets agreed upon should be carried on.

(4) In preparation for the primary role allotted, that of protection, intensive reconnaissance of German preparations for demolitions should be carried out, and plans made for counter action.

(5) SOE/FO will arrange to strengthen the resistance movement by the dispatch at the earliest possible opportunity of the maximum number of trained personnel from U.K."[218]

# Chapter 13

## CONCLUSION

**In the early summer of 1944** the Norwegian home forces could look back on four years of resistance against the Germans and the *Nasjonal Samling*. From scattered beginnings the force had grown to include in the military organization some 32,000 men.[219] Their work had not been easy, but their example had not gone unnoticed. His Majesty the King said in a speech to the Norwegian people on June 6, 1944, "The members of those organizations that work with the Allied military authorities, stand in a special place. They have received particular problems to solve and they will receive new orders."[220] There was no doubt that the home forces were ready and willing to take on new assignments. They were willing to sacrifice their lives, as many had done.

Consider the real meaning and worth of the resistance in Norway.

Before April 9, 1940, the Norwegian people had for generations lived in peace. It is perhaps safe to say that the average Norwegian had come to think of peace as a normal and lasting part of Norwegian life. The German attack came as a shock and led to a dramatic change in their accustomed life. The mental attitude, from that of peace to that of war, could not change immediately. It took some time before people could gather their thoughts and devise a strategy that was to become the main line of Norwegian occupation history, i.e., resistance against the Germans and the *Nasjonal Samling*.

### 1940-1941: The Learning Years

Improvisation and trial and error characterized the years 1940-1941. They can be called the learning years. The Norwegians were on the whole too trusting, too open and too talkative, too candid with their friends. The British, on the other hand, were forced to accept the criticism leveled at them by the Norwegians. The Norwegians claimed that the British were following a dangerous and too-independent course in

Norway, that, through raids, brought reprisals against the civilian population and made it extremely difficult for the resistance to do its work. Both the Norwegians and British seemed in the first years, to under-rate their opponents, first the Germans, and secondly the Norwegian collaborators. As a result, the military resistance was hard hit by arrests and deaths, and the civilian population was hard hit by reprisals. At the end of 1941, both Milorg and SOE saw that much of their work for a year and a half had not resulted in a significant impact against the German occupiers. A bitter Norwegian-British conflict over methods and means of conducting the war in Norway did not make mutual understanding any easier.

## 1942: The Resistance Grows

In 1942, the resistance gathered strength. The British were insistent upon making Norway "a thorn in the German side," more so since there were plans for an invasion. The potential strategy to cut Norway in half, Operation Jupiter, led to the tragedy at Majavatn in 1942. The civilian population suffered as a result of such operations which could not be pushed through to successful conclusions, such as at Majavatn and Telavåg. In the fall of 1942, SOE changed its outlook to a certain extent, and towards the end of 1942 and early 1943 one can rightly begin to speak of "a" resistance movement under "a" leadership, with a unified goal in mind.

1942 was also a big year for the civil resistance. The actions of Milorg and SOE certainly caused the *Gestapo* and *Abwehr* to be greatly concerned. The civilian resistance defeated the attempts by Quisling and the Germans to Nazify the Norwegian people. The Germans also realized that Quisling would never be a popular leader of the Norwegian people. The civilian resistance also came to stand beside the military resistance, so that by the end of 1942 they were more united than they had been at any previous time. Also, at this time these two groups came into closer cooperation with the Norwegian government in London and with the Allied leadership.

## 1943: Norway in the Shadow of the Great War

In 1943 it became clear to both the Norwegians and British that Norway was to be in the shadow of the Great War. Milorg was to "go slow and lie low." Milorg was to build itself in all the districts and it was decided that sabotage, rather than massive raids by air, was perhaps the best, most effective, and cheapest means of damaging the Germans in Norway.

## 1944: Formalization of Civilian and Military Cooperation

The first half of 1944 saw a formalization of the cooperation between the civilian and military arms of the resistance. The "Magna Carta" of the resistance, that was approved by the Norwegian government and was to have a real shape and substance to the Home Front, came into being.

Groups such as Milorg and *Kompani Linge* were recognized and sanctioned by the Norwegian government and found their place in the highest Allied plans for Norway. The home forces, by the summer of 1944, organized some 32,000 men into a fighting organization. In compliance with the June directive of 1944 from SHAEF, they grew stronger and by the Liberation were able to muster some 40,000 men, most of whom were well-trained, well-equipped and possessed of good morale.[221]

## Final Question: "Of What Value was the Resistance?"

This brief review of the primary organization and activities of the resistance leads us to a final question: "Of what value was the resistance?"

The resistance was a manifestation of a strong Norwegian will and desire to stand together in a time of national need. Certainly, there were disagreements, but none that destroyed the essential fabric of the entire resistance. The resistance movement agreed upon the essential goal, the destruction of Nazism. It worked to aid thousands of persons to flee the country, it aided those in need, it warned persons about to be arrested, and in general carried on nationwide humanitarian work. There was something fine and good about the work that was done, and there are those who, strange as it may seem, look back, not in horror, upon the experience as one of the richest periods of their lives.

It is hard to see how the occupation would have unfolded without the resistance to prod people along in opposition to the New Order. The resistance helped to keep young people from being taken in by the Nazis and NS. Also, the resistance gave the Norwegians a great deal of pride in the liberation that they had been active in bringing about. The liberation was not simply the result of actions by powers, but also the result of their own work. This is verified by SHAEF with regard to the disruption of railway traffic in Norway. Also, the resistance made the Norwegians more defense-minded. *Heimevernet* (the home guard) can be seen as a direct outgrowth of the home forces and their work.[222]

The military resistance also helped Norway to gain Allied status. This was important for the smooth transition of power in Norway after the war. The legal government was very shortly in power after the Germans capitulated. Also, Norway had a say in wartime reparations, war crime trials, and the founding of the United Nations.

The resistance movement can also be given credit for the smooth return to the legally constituted power of government that took place in Norway, in contrast to difficulties in other occupied lands. The resistance and the government had cooperated during the war and this cooperation continued after the war as well. The elections held in the fall of 1945 did not produce the bitter results that similar elections produced in other countries.

The resistance should be credited for at least part of the order with which the German capitulation took place at the end of the war. The home forces saved much in the way of power stations, bridges, and other such objects of great national worth. They provided a police force during the transition period. They earned the thanks of the government, given them at the demobilization in the summer of 1945.

Our home forces came into being when the enemy stood at the pinnacle of his might and ruled unchecked over the land. It grew steadily and surely in spite of powerful efforts to crush it. It is a principle of Norwegian youth never to give up, no matter the odds, for healthy youth need to fight for freedom and right.

# ■ ENDNOTES ■

1. Kjeldstadli, Sverre, Hjemmestyrkene, Oslo, 1959. 153. abb. Hjemmestyrkene, also Goebbels Diary, at the Hoover Library, selections of which have been copied by Magne Skodvin for the Historic Institute at the University of Oslo

2. Norges Krig, 1940-1945, ed. by Sverre Steen, 3 Vols. (Oslo, 1947-50), III, 472-73, abb. Norges Krig.
E. H. Stevens, Ed. "Trial of Nikolaus von Falkenhorst." War Crimes Trial Series. Vol. VI, London, 1948-50

3. Forsvarsstabens krigstidsarkiv, 1940-45, Festiningen, Oslo, abb. FA and FAFO IV, FA FOIV nylle 15 mappe 13-

4. Regjenringen og Hjemmefronten. Oslo, 1948, doc. nrs. 28, 29, 30, 31. abb ROH.
Sunde, A. Menn i Mørket. Oslo, 1947

5. FA, "Report of Captain Birger Sjøberg."

6. Magnus Paulsen of Fellingfors North Norway, Interview. Taken on May 2, 1962, in the City Hall Trofors. * Sicherheitspolizie und der Sicherheitsdienst Aussenstelle

7. Lyng, John. Forraederits Epoke, Oslo, 1948. 16. abb. Lyng.

8. FA FOIV hylle 15, mappe 13-A-2, "Tysk Kontraspionasage. Nordlige Norge," case no. 3.

9. Lyng, 110-115.

10. Erling Grannes of Tangen Majavatn Interview. Taken on May 18, 1962 at Fagerstrondvien, Oslo.

11. Ibid.

12. ROH nrs. 37, 38, 39, 40.

13. Historisk Institutt University of Oslo. A written report dated November 6, 1942. From: Parteigenosse Hayemann, Einsatzstab, Reichskommissariat Norwega: To: Parteikanzlei der NSDAP, Hauptbefaehlhaber Pg. Friedrichs, Munchen 33, Fuhrerbau aa/C 002532/41.

14. FA hylle 20 mappe, "Samarbeidt SOE, Diverse Operasjoner."

15. Historisk Institutt. University of Oslo. Memos of interview with Col. J. S. Wilson, Chief of the SOE Norwegian section by Sverre Kjeldstali: These memos will be referred to in subsequent footnotes only as Wilson.

16. Hjemmestyrkene, 166.

17. On October 6, 1942, fifteen men were shot. Peder Oddvar Stortjonnli, Oddvar Olsen, Magnus Lien, Edward Saeter, Peder Lundsaeter, Arne Holmen, Mikal Holmen, Aksel Johansen, Ingvald Mellingen, Tormod Iverland, Leif Sjøfors, Bjørne Lien, Nils Moellersen, Arne Moen, Agnar Bofjellmo, Erling Paulsen, Birger Paulsen and Magnus Paulsen. On October 7 ten men were shot. Otto Skirstad, Henry Gleditsch, Harold Langhelle, Hirsch Kommissar, Hans Konrad Ekornes, Gunnar S. Birch, Per T. Lykke, Gunnar Bull Aakrann, Peder Eggen and Finn Berg. October 8, nine men were shot. Johan Audan Bogfjellmo, Johan Oeygard, Einer Oeygard, Ole Saeter, Olaf Svebak, Alf Stormo, Emil Oyum, Pter Forbergskog, Rasmus Skjerpe.

18. Lyng, 25 ff. especially 39.
FA FOIV hylle 15 mappe 13-A-2. "Tyskkontraspionasje: Nordlige Norge," report fo a Thorvald Moe.

19. Nazi Conspiracy and Aggression. Office of U.S. Chief of Counsel for Prosecution of Axis Criminality. Vol. III. U.S. Govt. Printing Office, Washington, 1946-47. 431-33. (PS-508) and 433-34 (PS-512).

20. Voices of History, 1941-46, ed. by F. Watts and N. Ausubel. New York, 1942-1946, 433.

21. Hjemmestyrkene, 169. The organization of Milorg will be taken up in detail in Chapters IV and V.

22. See works on prelude to April 9, 1940. See particularly M. Skogvin's work Footnote #27.

23. Olsen, Kr. Anker. Norsk Hydro Gjennom 50 84. Oslo, 398.

24. FA lists of "Documents captured by British Land Forces in Norway (BLFN) after May 7, 1945." List No. 12 Serial No. 910,

deals with a shipping office established in Aalesund established April, 1940.
Report of John Olssen, undated. "An account of my experiences from shortly before the German invasion of Norway to my escape about six weeks later. Copy of the Historisk Institutt.

25. Hjemmestyrkene, 55.

26. Magne Skodvin, "German and British-French Plans for Operations in Scandinavia, 1940." The Norseman, IX (Nov:Dec., 1951). 372, abb. Skodvin, "German and British-French Plans."

27. Halvdan Koht. "Mr. Winston Churchill and the Norwegian Question." The Norseman, VIII (March - April, 1950), 78. abb. Koht. "Mr. Winston Churchill."

28. Skodvin. "German and British-French Plans." 35.

29. Ibid.

30. Koht, "Mr. Winston Churchill," 76.

31. Christensen, A. R., "Norway and World War II" in The Norway Yearbook, ed. J. Chs. Gunderson, (Oslo, 1950, 80-100.

32. Koht, "Mr. Winston Churchill," 80.

33. Koht, "Mr. Winston Churchill," 80.

34. Ibid., 80.

35. Ibid., 81.

36. Winston Churchill, The Second World War, 6 vols. (London 1948), vol I, 420. abb. Churchill II.

37. Koht, "Mr. Winston Churchill," 82.

38. Malcolm Munthe. Sweet is War (London, 1954), 53-89. abb. Munthe.

39. Ibid., 68 ff.

40. Ibid., 123 ff. and 214 ff and 217 ff.

41. Ibid., 214 ff and 217 ff.

42. Churchill II, Vol. II, 219.

43. Ibid., 218.

44. This operation took place before the existence of the SOE, but it is considered to be an SOE operation nevertheless.

45. Haukelid, K. Kampen om tungtvannet, Oslo, 1953, 11.

46. Hjemmestyrkene. 356.

47. Churchill II, Vol. II, 219.

48. Munthe, 120 ff.

49. The British resistance under "The Battle of Britain" in September, 1940, became a stimulus for the Norwegian will to resist.

50. Haestrup, J., Kontakt med England 1940-43, Koebenhavn, 1954, 75-77.

51. Munthe, 124 ff.

52. Ibid., 124 ff.

53. Ibid., 131 ff.

54. Buckley, C. Norway-The Commandos -Dieppe. London, 1951. abb. Buckley.

55. Hjemmestyrkene, 61.

56. Ibid., 40. "Ja vi elsker dette lande" is the first line of the Norwegian national anthem. This phrase is often translated as "yes, we love with fond devotion" however, the author feels that the direct translation "Yes, we love this land" is better suited to the case in point.

57. Letter from Churchill to Sir Roger Keyes, a copy of which was given S. Kjeldstadli by commander Frank Skagg and which was with the Kjeldstadli papers at the Historisk Institutt in Oslo. "The unqualified success of CLAYMORE says much for the care and skill with which it was planned, and the determination with which it was executed. Pray accept for yourself and pass to all concerned."

58. F. A. hylle 20, mappe "Samarbeidet med SOE Generelt."

59. F. A. hylle 20, mappe "Samarbeidet med SOE Generelt."

60. F. A. hylle 20, mappe "4-B-2."

61. Kompani Linge, I and II, Oslo, 1948. Foreward.

62. M. Skodvin, "Norsk okkupasjons historie; europeish samanheng." Nordisk Tidskrift XXXV (No. 6, 1951), 318. abb. Skodvin "Norskokk."

63. Ibid., 312.

64. Buckley, 186. "In mid-July M. Molotov had approached Sir Stafford Cripps, then British Ambassador to Moscow, with a proposal for joint action to occupy Spitzbergen and expel the Germans from northern Norway." 193. "... attention was given to a plan for establishing a quasi-permanent base for our own raiders either at Bodoe on the mainland or on one of the islands."

65. Ibid., 193.

66. Buckley, 193.

67. Ibid., 164, ff. "The mistake, if mistake there was lay in the tendency to prolong the pin-prick raids beyond the period when they formed the only offensive potential of our ground troops against northwestern Europe."

68. Ibid., 187.

69. Magne Skodvin, interview.

70. Ibid. also F. A. hylle 20.

71. Christense, Chr. A. R. "Okkuposjonsarog Etter-krigstid" Vaart Folks Historie (Oslo, 1961) IX, p. 293.

72. Buckley, 166. "The welcome extended by the population was warm so long as it appeared that our troops were making preparations for a prolonged and possibly permanent stay."

73. Straffesak mot Vidkun Abraham Lauritz Quizling, published by Eidsivating lagstol landssvik avedeling, Oslo, 1946.

74. Vaart Folks Historie IX, 294.

75. Buckley, 194. "Admiral Hamilton took the decision to withdraw during the afternoon, since the advantage of remaining a short time longer in these waters could not outweigh the danger of his ships that might result from dive-bombing attacks from hostile aircraft. [On the morning of December 28 a single German aircraft had dropped a bomb.]

76. Skodvin, "Norsk okk," 313.

77. Ibid., 316.

78. Skodvin, "Norsk okk," 314.

79. Robert Major Chief of the Forskning Raadet (Research Council) Oslo. University of Oslo formerly Capt. of Intelligence. Order of Battle Group Norwegian High Command. Robert Major states there were about 366,000 Germans in Norway at the time of the capitulation. 193,000 Army, 47,000 Air Force, 50,000 Navy and 16,000 S.S. plus other forces. An interview May 19, 1962.

80. Skodvin, "Norsk okk," 313.

81. Ibid., 313.

82. Vaart Folks Historie, IX, 173.

83. Schjelderup, Ferdinand, Fra Norges kamp for retten. 1940 i Hoeyesterett. (Oslo, 1945) (Norway's fight for justice. 1940 in the Supreme Court). Entire work.

84. FA, FO IV. From a document at the University of Oslo Historiske Institutt.

85. "In the spring of 1941 Harald Nordgarden of Mosjoen spoke with the undersigned about the possibility of finding some dependable men from the area to join in resistance against the Germans, and at the same time help in the event of an Allied invasion. It was at that time discussed how many Krag rifles had been hidden from the Germans and not been surrendered. The problem of how best to guard these weapons was also discussed. It proved to be that not one rifle of the Krag type had been delivered to the Germans from the area. That is to say that at each home there was at least one and possibly two Krag rifles." "We set up a group of men into a troop, the count totaled about twenty men besides myself, and in order not to arouse suspicion we carried out a program of organized gymnastics. At about Christmas time, 1941, four men came to Grane from England and began to organize weapons transport into the area. We of the home-forces received orders from our leader, Dr. Nissen Meyer, not to have anything to do with these people or the Norwegians that they were organizing for among these so-called good Norwegians were those who could not keep a secret." Full text in Appendix 3.

86. From the farewell speech of General Ruge at the time of capitulation by the Norwegian forces in Norway of June 10, 1940. A copy is to be found at the University of Oslo Historiske Institutt.

87. Skodvin, Magne, Interview.

88. Smaalaas, Vidar. Interview on May 2, 1962 at Majavatn. Vidar Smaalaas was a corporal (troppesjef 1 H.S.) See document in Appendix III. Rapport fr Smaalaasen tropp av Heimestyrkene i Namsskogan.

89. Smaalaas, Vidar. Interview. North Norwegian Association. West Norwegians League.

90. Hauge, Jens Christian. Interview on June 20, 1962, at Oslo. Mr. Hauge was a member of Raadet, HL, a leader of HS and a postwar Minister of Justice for Norway. At the present time he is an attorney in Norway.

91. Norges Krig, Vol. III, 7-34.

92. ROH. 39.

93. Ibid. 39.

94. Vaart Folks Historie, IX, 228-29.

95. Ibid., IX, 229.

96. Skodvin, Magne. An unpublished paper on the membership of the NS in Norway. 5-6. A table from 8/27/40 to 5/1/42. Less than 7000 of the 60,000 members in the NS files at the time of liberation had been NS members on October 1, 1940. On August 27, 1940 the membership stood at 4202, it reached a peak in November, 1943 at 43,400 and by October, 1944, the NS had lost about 1000 members. These figures do not include the youth organizations and the auxiliary organizations. These figures are a far cry from the 1939 boasts by Quislings of 200,000 to 300,000 followers and a solid membership of 15,000.

97. ROH, 50-59.

98. Instillingen fra Undersoekelseskommisjonen av 1945. Published by Stortinget (Parliament) 3 Vols. Oslo, 1947.

99. Magne Skodvin interview.

100. ROH, 8.

101. Ibid., 67.

102. Ibid., 7-8.

103. Ibid., 54, 60 and UK 1945, John Rognes.

104. Ibid., 7-9.

105. ROH, 8 and 42-44. Also see UK 1945, Jacob Schive, Report of February 3, 1947 about Raadet's relationship with the British and the Norwegian government.

106. Ibid., 42-44.

107. U.K. 1945, John Rogness, January 27, 1947.

108. ROH, 46. Directive to the Military Organization in Norway in reply to their Report dated the 10th of June, 1941 and addressed to H. M. King Haakon. Unsigned.

109. Ibid., 46.

110. Ibid., 49.

111. Nygaardsvold, J.: Beretning om den norske regjerings virksomhet fra 9. April 1940 til 25. Juni. Stortinget Oslo, 1947. 25. Clarification of the Norwegians Government's work from April 9, 1940 to June 25.

112. U.K. 1945, Vol. VI, 54-79.

113. Ibid., 57-58.

114. ROH, 49.

115. U.K. 1945, Jacob Schive, February 3, 1947.

116. ROH, 71-77.

117. Ibid., 77.

118. Hjemmestyrkene, 368, also ROH, 45-49.

119. Lie, T. Med England i ildtiden, 1940-42. Oslo, 1956. 18 ff.

120. Ibid., 250 and 285.

121. Munthe, 122.

122. Lie, 250. "The cooperation between Economic Welfare and Sir Charles Nambro and myself had begun as soon as I came to London."

123. Churchill II, Vol II, 572. Aletter of 7/23/40 to Eden.

124. Hjemmestyrkene, 92-93.

125. Skodvin interview. During the first months of 1941 there was a tendency for the local Milorg groups to look to Oslo for leadership. This tendency, while commendable in one way, led to too much information being known to too many people. This led to the arrests in the fall of 1941.

127. Lie, 251.

128. Hjemmestyrkene, 101-102.

129. F. A. hylle 20, folio, "Samarbeidet med SOE Generelt." Report dated January 14, 1942. "Problem of the Norwegian Independent Company."

130. Lie, 389.

131. Skodvin interview.

132. Skodvin. An unpublished paper on the membership of NS, 2-4. Skodvin states that while Quisling claimed a membership of some 15,000 and between 200,000 to 300,000 sympathizers the actual figures are much smaller. August 27, 1940, there are about 4,202 members and membership reached its peak in November, 1942 at 43,400 and went down from then on.

133. Skodvin interview and Historiske Institutt and Meddelelse fraa Riksadvokaten.

134. Hjemmestyrkene, 114, from SECRET. Prisoner of War Interrogations (PWSI) 269 reports. Report No. 120, entitled "Kjell Kvaloe Norwegian Citizen." Employed by AST Norway and SIPO and SD, Norway.

135. Hjemmestyrkene, 117, from PWSI report No. 80.

136. Ibid., 117, from PWSI report No. 134.

137. Straffesak, 33-39.

138. Secret German Documents Seized During the Raid on the Lofoten Islands on the 4th March, 1941. HMSO., London, 1941. 23-26. Translation of "Ricktlinien."

139. Wiesener, A. Nordmenn foer tysk Krigsrett, 1940-1942. (Oslo, 1947). the entire volume deals with the problems faced by Norwegians arraigned before German military courts.

140. Skodvin interview.

141. Norges Krig, III, 452.

142. Ibid., 452-53.

143. Vidar Smaalaas interview and attached report, Appendix 3.

144. Matloff & Snell. Strategic Planning for Coalition Warfare, 1941-42, 100, 189, 235, 239, 244, 267, 269, 278, 310, 326

145. Martienssen, A. Hitler and His Admirals. London, 1948, 116-17, and Wilmot, C. The Struggle for Europe. London, 1952, 93.

146. Leahy, W.D., I Was There, London, 1950, 93-94.

147. Robert Major interview. Korgen Mountain. Blodvegen

147. Hjemmestyrkene, 133. The road work in North Norway was of use to the Germans in their retreat from Finland in 1944.

149. Hjemmestyrkene, 133.

150. Hjemmestyrkene, 135. From a work by Ole Borge in connection with the investigation after the war concerning German plans for Norwegian aluminum production. Original in the Domsarkiv. See pages 22-23.

151. Wilmot, 110.

152. North, J. Northwest Europe 1944-45: The Achievement of the 21st Army Group. London, 1953, 18. "Operation Dynamite" is discussed in this work as the predecessor of "Operation Jupiter." "Operation Dynamite" was planned May 5, 1941 with its goal "to establish a bridgehead in the Stavanger area."

153. Bryant, A. The Turn of the Tide. London, 1957. Selections on the professional militaries objections to Churchill's plans.

154. Martinssen, 144.

155. Brassey's Naval Annual, "Fuehrer Conferences on Naval Affairs, 1939-1945," London, 1948.

156. Erling Grannes interview.

157. Norges Krig II, 728.

158. Norges Krig II, 73, and "Trial of Nikolaus von Falkenhorst." War Crimes Trial Series, Vol. VI, Ed. by E. H. Stevens. Von Falkenhorst sent only a brief telegram to Quisling congratulating him, "I did not take part in the celebration of Q's enthronement at the AKERSHUS fortress, because I was indifferent to it, and a duty journey seemed more important to me."

159. Straffesak, 591-96.

160. Hjemmestyrkene, 142, from L. P. Lochner, Goebbels Tagebucher, 72 (Zurich, 1948).

161. Straffesak, 540-541, a speech of November 16, 1941.

162. Ibid., 544, a speech by Sverre Riisnaes at Lillestroem, Feb. 20, 1942.

163. These *"joessinglister"* were patterns of the Germans *"Positiv-und Widerstandskartel"* which were published by Sipo u. S.D 1940/45. The fall of 1940 Quisling ordered that opposition people should be listed. Rolf Fuglesang was given the job of compiling and circulating these lists for the NS Before the fall of 1943, some 20,000 to 30,000 persons were on the lists, according to county, but the lists were shortened in 1943-44, so that new lists in the spring of 1944 contained only 2,000-3,000 names. These lists went to the Germans and to Norwegian police and it was meant that these people would be watched and rendered harmless in the event of Allied action.

164. Wyller, Th. C. Nyordning of Motstand. En Framstilling og en Analyse av Organisasjonenes Politiske Funksjon under den tyske Okkupasjon. 25.9.1940-25.9.1942 (Oslo 1958) Entire work. Also, Wyller's Fra Okkupasjonens Maktkamp (Oslo 1953). Foreign Minister Cabinet Minister and Chief of the State Chancellery Head of the Party Chancellery State Commissioner for Norway

165. Hjemmestyrkene, 144-145.

166. Straffesak, 604, testimony of Ernst Zuechner.

167. Evensmo, S. Englandsfarere, (Oslo 1947), 84.

168. Hjemmestyrkene, 174.

169. F. A. hylle 20, mappe, "ANCC moeter. The ANCC held 36 meetings between 2/16/42 to 4/26/45. Group later included the OSS and was called "Anglo-Americano-Norwegian Collaboration Committee."

170. Hjemmestyrkene, 175.

171. Hjemmestyrkene, 175.

172. ROH, 124-126.

173. FA hylle 29, mappe 1 1/6 41-99373.

174. ROH, 61.

175. Jens Chr. Hauge, interview.

176. Ibid.

177. Vidar Smaalaas interview.

178. Skodvin interview.

179. Wilmot. This work gives a clear picture of the Allies growing strength 1943-45.

180. Hjemmestyrkene, 192.

181. Magne Skodvin, "Norges plassi Hitlers militaereplaner etter Juni 1940," Historisk Tidsskrift, XXXI (1949-1951) 452.

182. Skodvin "Norges plass." 455.

183. Ibid., 455.

184. Ibid., 455.

185. Ibid., 455.

186. Wilmot, 144.

187. Brassey, 379.

188. Churchill II, Vol. V, 608.

189. Jens Chr. Hauge interview.

190. Hjemmestyrkene, 214.

191. Kompani Linge, Vol. 1, 161-170.

192. Hjemmestyrkene, 221.

193. Ibid., 221-22.

194. Trondheim Nidaros, June 2, 1945, 1.

195. I tysk Krigsfangenskap. Norske Offisers Opplevelser: Polen og Tyskland 1942-1945, ed. by Bakken, Hallvardsand, Oslo 1950, 49. The orders for the arrest of the Norwegian officers are printed in this book. Officers who were members of the NS were exempt from the arrests.

196. Hjemmestyrkene, 261.

197. Magne Skodvin interview.

198. ROH, 109-111.

199. Ibid., 9-10, 242-246, 331 ff.

200. Ibid., 243.

201. Hjemmestyrkene, 306, also Jens Chr. Hauge interview.

202. ROH, 9-11, also Jens Chr. Hauge interview.

203. Hjemmestyrkene, 311-13.

204. ROH, 239-241.

205. Ibid., Doc. Nos. 129, 136, 138, 140, 141, 143, 147, 154, 157, 159, 160, 163, 165, 167, 171, 184, 185, 186, 201, 204, 219 and others.

206. ROH, 44, also Jens Chr. Hauge interview.

207. Historiske Institutt University of Oslo, photostatic copy.

208. ROH, 304-309.

209. ROH, 331-335, Doc. No. 183, also Jens Chr. Hauge interview.

210. ROH, Doc. No. 183.

211. ROH, Doc. No. 183.

212. Jens Chr. Hauge interview, also Hjemmestyrkene, 319.

213. Magne Skodvin interview.

214. Historiske Institutt, University of Oslo, partial copy of protocol of the meeting, also ROH, Doc. No. 244.

215. ROH, Doc. No. 244.

216. ROH, Doc. Nos. 226, 221 and 224.

217. Royal Norwegian Information Service, Release of May 19, 1944 (NKUB) found at Norsk Krigstrykksamling at the University of Oslo.

218. Historiske Institutt. University of Oslo, Photostatic copy

219. Magne Skodvin interview.

220. ROH, Doc. No. 231. The king's closing words were Countrymen: Hold together and be ready. Long live the United Nations. Long live freedom.

221. Magne Skodvin interview.

222. Magne Skodvin interview.

**Photo Sources:**

Elting, John R., *Battles For Scandinavia*. (1967, Time-Life Books, Inc., New York).

Dildy C. Douglas, *Campaign: Denmark and Norway, 1940*. (New York, Oprey Publishing, 2007).

Steen, Sverre, Editor. *Norges Krig: 1940-1945*, (Oslo: Gyldendal Norsk Forlag, 1947). 3 Volumes.

# ◼ ARCHIVES AND BIBLIOGRAPHIES ◼

Boeninger, H.R. *The Hoover Library Collection on Germany.* Stanford, 1955.

*Guide to Captured German Documents.* Prep. By G. Weinberg and the W.D.P. Staff under the Direction of F.T. Epstein. Maxwell Air Force Base, Alabama, 1952.

Roberts, H.S. *Foreign Affairs Bibliography. A selected and annotated List of Books on International Relations. 1942/1945.* New York, 1955.

University of Oslo. *List of Books on Military Operations in Western Europe 1939/45.* Imperial War Museum. London, 1952.

Leahy, W.D. *I was there.* London, 1950.

Carlyle, M. *Documents on International Affairs.* 1939-1946.

Deane, J.R. *The Strange Alliance. The Story of our Efforts of Wartime Cooperation with Russia.* New York, 1947.

McNeill, W.H. *America, Britain and Russia; their Cooperation and Conflict 1941-1946.* London, 1953.

*Nazi-Soviet Relations 1939-1941, Documents from the Archives of the German Foreign Office.* Ed. by R.I. Sontag and J. S. Beddie. Washington, 1948.

Newmann, W.L. Making the Peace 1941-1945. *The Diplomacy of the Wartime Conferences,* Washington, 1950.

Weinberg, G.L. *Germany and the Soviet Union, 1939-1941.* Leiden, 1954.

## WAR STRATEGY

Craig, G.A. *The Politics of the Prussian Army 1940-1945.* Oxford University Press, 1955.

Gilbert, F. *Hitler directs his War. The Secret Records of his daily Military Conferences.* New York, 1951.

Martienson, A. *Hitler and his Admirals.* London, 1943.

Taylor, T. *Sword and Swastika. The Wehrmacht in the Third Reich.* London, 1953.

Wheeler-Bennet, J.W. *The Nemesis of Power. The German Army in Politics 1918-1945.* London, 1954.

## WARTIME OPERATIONS

Armstrong, T. *The Northern Sea Route.* London, 1952.

Assmann, K. "The Invasion of Norway" *U. S. Naval Institute Proceedings. April, 1952,* pp. 401-13.

Derry, T.K. *The Campaign in Norway.* London, 1952.

Edwards, K. *Operation Neptune.* London, 1946.

Frischauer, P.V. & Jackson, R. *The Altmark Affair.* New York, 1955.

Hackett, J.W. "The Employment of Special Forces." *Journal of the Royal United Service Institutions.* Feb. 1952. Pp26-41.

Norman, A. *Operation Overlord. Design and Reality. The Allied Invasion of Western Europe.* Harrisburg, Penn. 1956.

## GENERAL WORKS ON THE WAR

Churchill, W.S. *The Second World War.* 6 Vols. London, 1948-54.

Eisenhower, D.D. *Crusade in Europe.* Doubleday and Company, 1948.

Fuller, J.F.C. *The Second World War 1939-45. A Strategical and Tactical History.* London, 1948.

*Voices of History, 1941-46.* Ed. by F. Watts and Ausubel. New York, 1942-46.

Wilmot, C. *The Struggle for Europe.* London, 1952.

## INFORMATION FROM POST-WAR INVESTIGATIONS

DeJong, L. *The German Fifth Column in the Second World War.* London, 1956.

Miksche, F. O. *Secret Forces. The Technique of Underground Movements.* London, 1950.

Schellenberg, W. *The Schellenberg Memoirs. A Record of the Nazi Secret Service.* London, 1957.

## WAR CRIMES

Albrecht, A.R. "War Reprisals in the War Crimes Trial and in the Geneva Convention of 1949." *American Journal of International Law.* (Oct. 1953) 590-6171.

Office of U.S. Chief of Counsel for Prosecution of Axis Criminality. *Nazi Conspiracy and Aggression.* 8 Vols. Washington, 1946-47.U.S. Gov. P.O.

Trial of Nikolaus von Falkenhorst. *War Crimes Trial Series.* Vol. VI, Ed. by E.H. Stevens.

## OCCUPATION AND RESISTANCE

Almond, F.A. "The Resistance and the Political Parties of Western Europe." *Political Science Quarterly.* LXII (1947) 27-61.

*Conditions in Occupied Territories.* A Series of Reports issued by the Inter-Allied Information Committee. London, 1942. Nos. 1-6.

Glahn, G. von. The Occupation of Enemy Territory. . . A Commentary on the Law and Practice of Belligerent Occupation. University of Minnesota Press. 1957.

Steinbeck, J. *The Moon is Down.* New York, 1942.

Wuorinen, J.H. *Finland and World War II 1939-1944.* New York, 1948.

## INTERVIEWS

Grannes, Erling. Retired. Formerly a farmer at Tangen, Majavatn. Interviewed May 18, 1962.

Hauge, Jens Christian. Attorney. Formerly Minister of justice and before that a leader of the Norwegian resistance as member of Rådet, H.L. Chief of H.S. Interviewed June 20, 1962.

Haukaas, Kaare. Law faculty University of Oslo and Curator Norsk Krigstrykk Samling Universitets Biblotek. Oslo. Interview October 1961 and June 1962.

Major Robert. Chief of the Oslo Forsknigs Rådet. Blindern, Oslo, May 19, 1962.

Paulson, Magnus. Truck driver in Fellingfors. Active in Resistance. Transported weapons by truck from Mosjøen. Interviewed in Trofors May 2, 1962.

Pøien, Per. Editor for Adressavisen, Trondheim. Interviewed May 4,1962.

Skodvin, Magne. Professor Historisk Institutet. University of Oslo. Continuing interviews and consultation for the entire period September, 1961 to June 1962.

Smalås, Vidar. Saw mill owner. Formerly leader of Smalåsen troop of Milorg. Interviewed Majavatn May 2, 1962.

Solbaken, Andres. Owner of a men's store in Mosjøen.

Svare, Reider. Manager of the Vefsen Sparebank of Mosjøen, Norway. Now the local historian for the area encompassing Mosjøen and outlying Granne Herred, including Majavatn, Vefsen, and Vistenfjord. May 2, 1962.

# ■ APPENDIX 1 ■

## List of abbreviations and foreign terms used in text and notes

| Abbreviation/Term | English Definition |
| --- | --- |
| *Abwehr* | German military intelligence organization |
| ANCC | Anglo Norwegian Collaboration Committee |
| AOK *(Armee-Oberkommando)* | Army High Command |
| BBC | British Broadcasting Company |
| B-org *(Bedriftsorganisasjonen)* | Industrial Organizations |
| CCO | Chief of Combined Operations |
| DCO | Directorate of Combined Operations |
| Domsarkiv-Oslopolitikammer | Judicial records Oslo Police |
| FA *(Forsvarsstabens Krigstidarkiv 1940-45)* | Defense staff wartime records. Akershus Fortress, Oslo |
| FD *(Forsvarsdepartementet)* | Defense Department |
| FO *(Forsvarets Overkommando)* | Defense Command |
| FO IV *(Forsvarets Overkommando Dept. IV)* | Dept IV, Defense Command Dept. IV London 1942-45 |
| FO IV *(Forsvarets Overkommando)* | Defense Command Dept. IV London. 1942-45 |
| Fo-H *(Forsvarets Overkommando, Hjemmegruppen)* | Defense Command Homegroup London 1941-45 |
| Fylke | County |
| Gestapo *(Die Geheime Staatspolizei)* | Secret police of Nazi Germany |
| Grepo *(det norske (NS) Gresepoliti)* | Norwegian Border Police, *Nasjonal Samling*, during the occupation |
| HHI *(Hjemmerfrontens Historieinstitutts arkiv)* | The Homefronts Historical records. Akershus Fortress. Oslo |
| HL *(Hjemmefrontens Ledelse)* | Homefronts Leadership |
| HOK *(Haerens Overkommando)* | Army High Command |
| HS *(Hjemmestyrkene)* | Home forces |
| Joessing lister | Lists drawn up by the NS of persons suspected of anti-NS activity |
| KK *(Koordinasjoneskommiteen)* | Coordination Committee HS |
| M.IV *(Militaer Kontoret, IV)* | Military Office IV at the Royal Norwegian Legation in Stockholm |
| Milorg *(Militaer organisasjonen)* | Military Organization in Norway 1940-45 |
| NDSAP | Nazi Party |
| NORICEN | Norwegian Independent Company (No. 1) also called *Kompany Linge* |
| NS *(Nasjonal Samling)* | The Quisling Nazi party |
| OKH *(das Oberkommando des Heeres)* | Nazi Germany's High Command of the Army from 1936 to 1945 |
| OKM *(das Oberkommando der Marine)* | Nazi Germany's Naval High Command |
| OKW *(das Oberkommando der Wehrmach)* | Part of the command structure of the armed forces *(Wehrmacht)* of Nazi Germany |
| OSS | Office of Strategic Services |
| R *(Rådet)* | Milorg's Council |
| RK | der Reichskommissar |
| RS *(Rad Sivil)* | Civil Council |
| RSO *(Riksarkivets samlinger)* | State records, Oslo |
| SHAEF | Supreme Headquarters of Allied Expeditionary Forces |
| Sipo *(det norske [NS] Sikkerhets politi)* | Norwegian Secret Police during the occupation |
| SIS | Secret Intelligence Service |
| Sipo u. SD *(die Sicherheitspolizei und der Sicherheitsdienst)* | The police and intelligence-gathering organization responsible for repression of the local population and for the persecution of the resistance, Communism and the Jewish population |
| Sivilorg *(Sivilorganisasjonen)* | Civil Organization of HS |
| SL *(Sentralledelsen Milorg)* | Milorg's Central Leadership |
| SOE | Special Operations Executive |
| Stapo *(det norske [NS] Statspoliti)* | Norwegian State Police during the occupation. |

# ■ APPENDIX 2 ■

## District Organization

Milorg Directive Number 1, promulgated in the spring of 1942, laid the groundwork for the command structure in Milorg that, with refinements, lasted throughout the war. Central Leadership (SL) established a structure of districts numbered from 11 through 24. District 14 was later subdivided into 14.1, 14.2, and 14.3; further a part of District 15 was added to 14.1. District 18 was divided into 18.1 and 18.2, and District 20 became 20.1, 20.2, and 20.3. District 25 was created from District 23, and District 26 came from District 24.

Directive Number 1 laid out the staff organization for each district as follows:
▶ district chief and staff
▶ battle groups
▶ communications, information, medical, supply and activity units
▶ national police

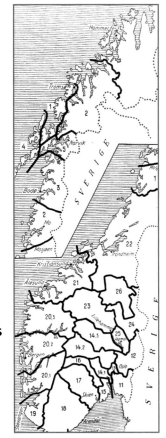

Each district should be divided into two to four sections with a section leadership. The sections should be subdivided into two to four areas, each with a leader. Each area should have two to four companies. A company should consist of two to four troops which would be organized into two to four squads with six to twelve men each. The three counties of northern Norway were designated as districts 1 - 5.

■ **Map of the 26 Milorg districts**

# ■ APPENDIX 3 ■

## Report from Smalåsen Tropp of Heimstyrkene in Namskogan.

In the spring of 1941, Harald Nordgård, of Mosjøen talked with the undersigned to see if he could find some dependable men in the area, who wanted to belong to the resistance against the Germans. It was then discussed how many Krag riffles were hidden and could be used and were not damaged. It was known that not a single Krag riffle from our area was turned in. This meant that there were one or two Krag riffles on every farm. At Christmas time 1941, four men from England came to Grane and started to organize weapons transport. Our group was at that time organized by Gudmund Bjørnstad, who belonged to the organization at Namskogan with Dr. Nissan Meyer as leader. He made it clear to us that we could not join the men from the north because they were not careful enough. The problem was that among the so-called good Norwegians, there were those who could not keep a secret. I became the contact person for the organization at Majavatn and here at Namskogan. My contact at Majavatn was Nils Møllersen. He was shot at Falstad in the fall of 1942, but he had been able to not leak any information to the interrogation. Otherwise it would have been bad for the people living there.

During the summer of 1942, the men from England living at Majavatn got organized like us. A report about this is given by R.C. Hansen. In the late summer of the same year, (the organization at Majavatn was in ordinary conversation among people who knew what was going on). But Nissen Meyer felt that there was nothing else to do but to put the organization "on ice" until later. During the fall of 1942, the catastrophe happened at Majavatn. The organization saved one of the guys from England who had been taken by the Gestapo. Many of them were sent to Falstad. Falstad was where many of the prisoners were executed. The reason that I was arrested was that one of the guys from Grane had completely broken down under torture and gave all of his information. He was one of my contact men, but none of the other men from our organization were arrested at that time.

I was arrested with three men from Majavatn. We were each given a spade and told to dig our own grave. After that the Germans asked if we knew that we had dug our own graves. It got so bad in the meantime that we were driven to Majavatn to start our imprisonment. About 60 of us were placed in a tiny room where there was not even room to lay down on the floor. After that we were taken to Falstad where we were tortured and 23 Majavatn men were shot. "Greet the people at home" were the last words that those that were to be executed said.

Signed – Smalåsen the 8th of August 1946.

Vidar Smalås fhv troppsjet i H.S.

# ■ APPENDIX 4 ■

### Report from Reidar Årkvizlas 1942

Monday, the 9th of August 1942, late in the evening, Reidar Årkvislas came up to my room where Arne Østgaard and I sat. RÅ told the following: He had been arrested by the Gestapo on early Sunday, morning the 8th of August, at Alf Stormo's house in Trofors. There was also a "Norwegian" with the Gestapo, (that I later, with RÅ's description, recognized as the Gestapo agent Odd Randall now arrested in Mosjøen). RÅ was transported from Trofors to Majavatn and home to the Grannes farm where the house was searched. Some weapons and hand grenades were found. Grannes was arrested and they were both taken from there. RÅ was handcuffed together with a German and had a sack of hand grenades on his back.

Coming up the hill, they saw Kalle up in the woods. He waved to them and they threw themselves down. At the same time, they heard a loud noise from other machine guns up in the woods. They all rolled on the ground and Grannes knocked down the guard who was watching him and shot the German who was handcuffed to RÅ. This is how they both freed themselves. Afterward, he went to Mellingsdalen, near Mollingsvatnet, and then to Smalåsen. (It was full of German police there, about 60 men.) He first visited Arne Smalås, but was stopped by a German guard in the entryway who wanted to see his pass. RÅ then said that a person doesn't take his pass along to walk to a neighbor's to borrow a horse. Arne Smalås came along then, and he figured out what was going on and said he didn't want to loan his horse, but that he could check over at the neighbors. RÅ was allowed to go again. Then he came to me and told me the story so clearly that I can still remember it after such a long time.

RÅ was completely soaked and changed his clothes from head to foot; shoes, socks and pants. He ate like he had never eaten before, since he hadn't eaten for 48 hours and got a backpack with a pack lunch. After consultation with Arne Østgaard, I got a hold of signalman Kåre Sven. The Germans had stationed guards on all the bridges but had forgotten the railroad bridge over Namsen. After RÅ had rested for about two hours, we started at about midnight. It was very dark and it was raining like the heavens had opened. Very good weather for people who are being followed. Then we travelled to Namskogan station where we woke Gunnar and Sverre Sandstedt. We were supposed to get one of them to drive RÅ by car to Røyrvik and Huddingsdalne, but they explained that the German police had already gone that way. I then followed RÅ to a barn where he was to stay until he heard the first stanza of a specific song. Gunnar Sandstedt took it upon himself to warn Edv. Bjørhusdal, who was going to take care of the continuing travel to Sweden,.

It shouldn't be necessary to explain what it would have meant for us to have had a home defense in 1940 that had been as well organized as "Hjemmestyrkene (HS)." Up here in the north the Germans had only one way to come. It was the main road, number 50. Along with some of the HS who knew the area people in the woods here, I believe the German advance would have gone slowly northward and would have cost them a lot of blood and little for us. An advantage would have been that it would have taken only hours to put together a militia on the warpath.

# ■ INDEX ■